REDEFINING
SUCCESS

REDEFINING
SUCCESS

STILL MAKING MISTAKES

W. BRETT WILSON

PORTFOLIO
PENGUIN

PORTFOLIO PENGUIN
an imprint of Penguin Canada Books Inc.

Published by the Penguin Group
Penguin Canada Books Inc., 90 Eglinton Avenue East, Suite 700,
Toronto, Ontario, Canada M4P 2Y3

Penguin Group (USA) Inc., 375 Hudson Street, New York, New York 10014, U.S.A.
Penguin Books Ltd, 80 Strand, London WC2R 0RL, England
Penguin Ireland, 25 St Stephen's Green, Dublin 2, Ireland (a division of Penguin Books Ltd)
Penguin Group (Australia), 707 Collins Street, Melbourne, Victoria 3008, Australia
(a division of Pearson Australia Group Pty Ltd)
Penguin Books India Pvt Ltd, 11 Community Centre, Panchsheel Park, New Delhi – 110 017, India
Penguin Group (NZ), 67 Apollo Drive, Rosedale, Auckland 0632, New Zealand
(a division of Pearson New Zealand Ltd)
Penguin Books (South Africa) (Pty) Ltd, 24 Sturdee Avenue, Rosebank,
Johannesburg 2196, South Africa

Penguin Books Ltd, Registered Offices: 80 Strand, London WC2R 0RL, England

First published in hardcover by Penguin Canada, 2012
Published in this edition, 2013

1 2 3 4 5 6 7 8 9 10 (RRD)

Manufactured in the U.S.A.

LIBRARY AND ARCHIVES CANADA CATALOGUING IN PUBLICATION

Wilson, W. Brett, 1957–
Redefining success : still making mistakes / W. Brett Wilson.

ISBN 978-0-670-06694-0 (bound). – ISBN 978-0-143-18420-1 (pbk.)

1. Success in business. 2. Work-life balance. 3. Quality of life.
4. Wilson, W. Brett, 1957–. 5. Investment bankers—Canada—Biography.
6. Businessmen—Canada—Biography. I. Title.

HF5386.W54 2012   650.1   C2012-905854-8

Visit the Penguin Canada website at **www.penguin.ca**

Special and corporate bulk purchase rates available; please see
www.penguin.ca/corporatesales or call 1-800-810-3104, ext. 2477.

For my family

Contents

Thank You

Every book requires inspiration.

My first level of inspiration came from the folks closest to me on the roller coaster of my life journey, from my wonderful family, loyal personal friends and many great business partners to my trusting and dedicated staff. My second level of inspiration comes from a couple of dogs—yup, dogs—whose unconditional love and acceptance some days encourages and inspires me more than they could ever know or have known—thank you Maya and JCash.

I thank those around me for patiently—on most days—tolerating my idiosyncrasies, enduring my quirky habits and encouraging my dreams. I offer gratitude to each of Joni, Barb, Keith, Jeffrey, Robin, Emily and Jill for their respective and very different roles in bringing this book to reality. And to Hilary—two amazing pooches and I are most appreciative of all that you have done and continue to do for us.

Not everyone important to me is named or mentioned in this book, nor can they be: space simply doesn't permit. But, that said, I am grateful to each of you for the role you have taken in influencing the course of my unique life.

You know who you are.

Thank you,

Brett

PS: Dad, I love you. Mom, I miss you.
PPS: Second Mom, I love you, too.

Foreword
by Joni Avram

Not many people of Brett's stature or profile are so strikingly honest or open about their mistakes. Even fewer would write a book disclosing so many of them.

As one who has worked with Brett for many years, I know that part of his magic is his willingness to lay it all out there. As I've watched the ups and downs of his life from the sidelines, and helped him to grow in prominence on the national stage, I know that, more than anything, people connect with his humanity. While not everyone loves him, few would argue about the size of his heart. It's what motivates him to reveal things others would rather hide. And it's what makes him one of the most influential people of our time.

"You Have Two Minutes, Go!"

I was first introduced to Brett through a mutual friend in late 2006. At the time, he was just becoming known for his philanthropic work. His name barely showed up on a Google search. I tried for months to get a meeting with him. I began to realize he really wanted me to just politely go away. Instead, I bought a ticket to one of his public events. All the way there, I tried talking myself out of such a bold move. *He's going to think I'm stalking him!* But I decided I had nothing to lose. I saw him walk in, gave him some time to settle in and then caught him alone when he ordered a Coke at the bar. I tapped him on the shoulder and introduced myself. He remembered me and while, gracious, he wasted no time. "Okay," he said, "you have two minutes.

Go!" Nervous, I pulled my thoughts together and made my pitch about supporting his philanthropic work. I passed that quick test, but it was another month before the follow-up meeting at his FirstEnergy office. That meeting was also brief but he hired me that day. It was the beginning of one of the most inspirational journeys of my life.

Random Acts of Kindness

I've now worked with Brett for more than five years. The concept behind Brett's "serial philanthropy" is simple: it's about engaging others in the process of making the world better. Like Scrooge, who learned how to celebrate Christmas after years of miserliness, Brett seized the chance to encourage others to find significance (and happiness) within success after years of devoting the majority of his time to his business affairs.

There aren't many philanthropists who would take the time to organize sixty friends on a late December night to help feed the hungry. But he does. Year after year. He visits a local women's shelter every Christmas Day morning to share baking and stories. He gives people a chance to see how easy it is to make a big difference in the lives of others, and he does it right alongside them, pouring coffee and bussing tables. That's just one of the ways he plants seeds of inspiration in the hearts of others, and encourages them to follow his lead.

Tornadoes and Trailer Parks

For all the community work he does in private (which goes without notice) another side of Brett's philanthropy has been very public. I have sometimes joked that Brett is attracted to publicity the way tornadoes are attracted to trailer parks, but his enhanced profile has been strategic. It's one of the ways we have chosen to lever his social investments. As a hands-on philanthropist, he has not hesitated to show leadership. As Brett's fame has grown, so has his impact. Just ask any non-profit what it's like to have Brett advance their cause and they'll tell you it's like winning the lottery.

Some of what I most admire about Brett's work is what goes on behind the scenes. In addition to profile for the cause, Brett gives leaders in the non-profit space guidance on effective event design and marketing, challenges them to think beyond their current assumptions, and even makes his team available to support their efforts and enhance their effectiveness. Guests at his personal events often include war veterans, and the women and children living in shelters to escape abuse. The fact that Brett quietly includes them in his personal celebrations is another example of his generous heart. Brett's focus on people in every part of his life really is fundamental to his new definition of success.

"Hi, Dad, Will Call You Right Back"

One of the best examples of the value he places on people—especially family –happened not long ago, when Brett was speaking to hundreds of student leaders from across Canada at a national conference at the University of Calgary. When he was about halfway through his speech, talking about the importance of relationships with family and friends, his phone rang. He paused to turn the ringer off, but instead answered it. "Hi, Dad," he said. "I am a bit busy now but I'll call you right back." The significance of that little gesture was not lost on the crowd. Brett's dad mattered as much as his public speaking platform. The kids loved it, and gave Brett a grateful round of applause for a life lesson they would remember.

Seeds and Flowers

Brett has been sowing seeds of inspiration from his huge heart for years. Those seeds, large and small, have taken root in the hearts of too many to count. This book is another one of those seeds. Having worked closely with Brett to help pull these pages together, I sincerely believe his story will inspire you to see your own potential for impacting the world, whether it's through your family, your business or your community work.

One of my all-time favourite "Brett moments" was watching him return to his hometown of North Battleford, Saskatchewan, for Brett Wilson Day—a day of thank-yous and appreciation for the way Brett had engaged the entire community in a new attitude towards giving. He stood on stage as representatives from some thirty organizations lined up to personally thank him for his gifts. Each person presented him with a single flower. Tears streamed down Brett's face as the bouquet grew, overwhelmed by the simple but so heartfelt affection of the people his generosity had touched. There is no better picture for me of Brett Wilson's successful life—redefined.

Joni Avram, JD, is a consultant working with donors and charities to maximize both impact and engagement. (www.causeeffect.ca)

Introduction

I often encounter people searching for "the secret"—that one piece of advice—that will help them to jump ahead of their competition in the pursuit of success. Almost daily, I receive impassioned requests for partnership or investment from people wanting to move ahead as entrepreneurs or philanthropists or to simply have me act as their mentor or coach. People almost always want to know what I did to become successful.

What was it that enabled me to become one of Canada's top investment bankers, in one of the most ruthlessly competitive industries in the world, before I was forty years old? Was it luck or timing? Was it guts or determination? Was it an unrelenting competitive spirit? Was it book smarts or street smarts? Was it a strong moral compass to guide me to what is right and what is wrong? Was it my purportedly vast network of contacts? Or was it my often wise and fortunate selection of partners in almost every aspect of my life? Were there a few crucial choices that made all the difference?

The answer is yes, to varying degrees, to all the above. But that's certainly not the whole story. There is so much more. My path to success—however you choose to define success—also included stumbling through a multitude of misplaced or misguided priorities, tripping into mistakes of all sorts in almost all aspects of my life, and basically encountering speed bumps or setbacks of every imaginable kind. While I do learn (or at least try to learn) from my mistakes, I have also accepted that making mistakes is simply part of my life. I believe I do learn from my mistakes, while trying not to repeat them more than once or twice.

For many years, I pursued business with an uncompromising focus: extreme passion, drive and commitment were the norm. I was so hungry for the next deal that I willingly worked seven days a week for fifty-one or more weeks a year. Yes, I lived for the next deal. And the next dollar. In the process of expanding my bank account and building my deal-making and investing skills, I literally walked away from my marriage, ignored my health in too many ways and was rarely home as my children were being raised. I learned the hard way that it's possible to achieve considerable financial success and the respect of my business peers, while almost losing those very things that truly matter most at the end of the day.

> *"The only man who never makes a mistake is the man who never does anything."*
> —Theodore Roosevelt

At present, I travel across the country talking about what I've come to understand about the real secrets of success in business and life as I see them. What have I learned and shared? That balancing and pursuing one's life passions within a clearly defined set of priorities is the key to living a life you can become very proud of. Paradoxically, I didn't begin to find enduring success until I learned to define success, not by the size of my wallet, my car, my vacation, my home or my office, but rather by the size of my smile and the smiles of those closest to me—the happiness factor.

The overwhelmingly positive response to my public speaking events has shown me that people care deeply about these same issues and often react by taking a good long look at how they live.

After one of my recent speeches, a businessman/husband/father who was moved by the experience emailed me. This is an extract from that email:

> I have a beautiful wife and two amazing little boys and can honestly say that up until today, work was ahead of them. I think that 90 percent of the problems in my marriage stemmed from me working all day and then coming home and working all night ….
>
> Shortly after your speech, I called my wife and apologized about the past. You said at the start of your speech that maybe we will start doing things differently tomorrow. I guarantee that things will be different in my life when I get home …

This email is one of hundreds I have appreciated receiving after sharing aspects of my journey at talks I have given. Feedback like this was the underlying motivation for writing this book. My goal is to inspire people to consider thinking, acting and living with a renewed commitment to a set of basic life principles. Principles such as truly caring for the people closest to you—for me that includes both life *and* business partners. Principles such as living according to a strong moral compass, which includes a commitment to honesty, trustworthiness, keeping your word, being respectful, giving back and following through on a promise. Principles such as finding a work/life balance that can sustain your health and relationships and provide for real, lasting happiness.

> "When I speak to various groups across the country, work/life balance strikes the biggest chord. Signing the latest business deal means almost nothing if you're rarely there to tuck your children in at night."—WBW

In short, I believe that if people are really going to find meaningful and relevant success, they have to begin by carefully defining what they mean by the term. They have to understand that happiness and success are at best only loosely connected. They need to see that material or financial success (or celebrity) does not lead to happiness, a fact that should be beyond doubt or question. I believe that anyone who truly understands and appreciates happiness will realize that the pursuit of happiness really does point the way to success in life and business. People who seek and find this happiness will enjoy life's journey to the fullest.

Today, I am inclined to evaluate my approach to success a little differently:

- I try to make all aspects of my health and my personal relationships my highest priorities.

- I try to live according to a set of ethical precepts and values that lets me sleep well at night (and still make money) knowing that my moral compass is always pointing towards doing what's right.

- I try to regularly seek, create and seize opportunities to make the world a little better than I found it.

"Come on, Wilson," I can imagine you will say. "Surely you can't be saying that the path to success in life and business is as simple as that?"

Actually, you would be right: it's not all that simple. It takes work and commitment to consistently live by a set of core values. But I have learned by trial and error (with emphasis on a *lot* of errors) that these simple virtues are the foundation for real success, both in business and life. It's not always an easy path. It's definitely not the only path. But I believe it's the best path. It is the path I have chosen. And that is what this book is about.

Thank you for joining me as I share my mistake-riddled, success-focused, roller-coaster journey of a life …

Here is a man training a kite.

Hand-painted silk, the texture of desire, spinners and spin-socks. Aloft, that alluring word, gale or breeze while the string tugs at the hand, inviting the kinetic release of flight. Kites tangle the wind, unafraid of updraft or space, the temptation of gust. Thermal breezes invent mythologies.

A kite rides wind-glow, follows prevailing westerlies or polar easterlies, bestride chinook and rain shadow and gales racing themselves down to breezes that can lift only whispers. The sun stands still, wind shear inspiring thunder or a song that blasts all surface clean.

A kite is a tethered wing that defies gravity. Aerial ballet dancing mystery, lofting signals, extracting currents from clouds. It alloys mystery and art, combines hope and agility, just waiting for a gust to lift the ground, the thin veil of conviction, the invitation of lightning. Glide and pulse, soar past all obstacles to shine, buoyant, aerostatic, nature's mystery in how the wind can lift the substantial from the solid.

Catch and release ladders promise escape, hatching the building toward a kite-flying sky clear as conscience, blue light fracturing brick and glass block, opaque and gestural. No getaway, the steps lead both up and down, yet nowhere.

Fly a kite into a tree as a metaphor for life's surprises. Fly a kite into a fire escape as a symbol of line, control and lift, balance and drag. A kite is heavier than air but lighter than dream, always non-compliant.

Time to fly a kite.

The man who flies a kite flies too. The man who flies a kite, flies too.

—Aritha van Herk

One

Wealth-Obsessed World

The idea that I might write a book first occurred to me in the fall of 2008, in the middle of one of the most challenging business climates (read "economic collapses") to prevail either in North America or Europe in decades. The big question on everyone's mind was then moving from, "How do we get out of this mess?" back to "How did we get in this mess in the first place?" As it has evolved, my personal journey addresses this very business-focused question. This is a journey that touches on many aspects of my own life, and challenges the status quo–thinking behind corporate decision making.

I decided to speak out on the apparent lack of moral leadership in the business world because I thought what was needed was a voice that suggested the end of the world was not upon us. Economies have always gone through cycles, and always will. I suggested that leaders at all levels of life and business needed to encourage a stay-the-course sense of optimism in the face of the extraordinary gloom-and-doom attitude adopted by much of the media and many politicians. I argued that our financial issues were not with the people doing the work, but rather with the people pulling the strings, the leaders of our so-called "Corporate America."

I have often spoken about the causes of the 2008 recession. I believed that what we faced—and what we still face to a degree—was not a strictly financial crisis, not the "crisis of credit" that the pundits pontificated about, but rather a crisis of morality, characterized by excessive greed, entitlement-based arrogance and misplaced priorities, all predicated on a completely distorted or delusional view of what it means to succeed. The true crisis was one of corporate leadership and of morality. The credit issues with sub-prime mortgages were serious, but to me they were but the straw that broke the camel's back.

I believe that business leaders, political leaders, community leaders and religious leaders as well have an ongoing and ever-increasing responsibility to stand up and inspire a new level of confidence in the business community by our citizens. People are disgusted by the corruption and greed they see in the headlines; this really is the perfect time to inspire a moral renaissance and a reassertion of some basic life principles and values.

How We Got Here

Most people are aware of the series of events that led to the almost global economic downturn that deepened in early 2009. Over-leveraged assets, especially personal homes, led to a virtual and disastrous collapse in global financial markets, all but destroying the American and European banking systems while hammering consumer confidence, consumption and demand, and therefore commodity prices. A death spiral for the capital markets. In many parts of the world, foreclosures greatly outpaced government efforts to stop them. The number of bankruptcies skyrocketed. Unemployment levels reached record highs. Thanks to a roller-coaster stock market, retirement savings dwindled just as baby boomers were hitting retirement age. But let me go back.

I'm one of those boomers. And it's not the first time I've weathered a boom-and-bust economy. Born in 1957 in the small prairie city of North Battleford, Saskatchewan, I studied civil engineering, worked as an oil field engineer, went on to earn an MBA, and began a tumultuous but very rewarding career as an investment banker focused on Canada's lucrative energy industry. I graduated with my engineering degree in 1979, barely a year before the federal government's ill-fated National Energy Program was announced in the fall of 1980 (yes, three-plus decades later, it's still that Liberal-driven economic program that Albertans love to hate). As the economic collapse in Alberta continued to deepen in 1981, the value of our house fell below the amount of our mortgage—my wife and I clearly had more debt than assets. Suddenly, we found ourselves effectively bankrupt, only a few short years out of engineering school. The yellow brick road was not paved with gold. And potholes were abundant.

"Even a mistake may turn out to be the one thing necessary to a worthwhile achievement."—Henry Ford

My wife and I worked hard just to cover costs for the next decade. It took many years to crawl out of that financial hole, but we did. The total collapse of the world price of oil in late 1985 didn't help generate any wealth either: this economic downturn came just as I graduated with my MBA from the University of Calgary and began my career as an investment banker. Eventually I went on to spend almost two decades as a partner building one of the country's most successful investment banks, FirstEnergy Capital Corp. I subsequently took the significant cash flow my investment-banking career generated and began investing in a wide variety of often very successful businesses, and donating a great deal of money to charity. By most measures, life should have been very good.

Then along came the fall of 2008. I should have seen the collapse in the economy coming—I recall vividly a business news story headline something like "Hummer Sales Plummet 50%" in April 2008. The world price of crude oil had driven the price of gasoline so high that even the most price-insensitive consumers of gasoline, Hummer owners, were throwing in the towel. One could only imagine the pain that others were feeling, or were about to feel. In hindsight, the collapse of the incredibly over-levered personal credit markets was inevitable. But I missed the signals. Maybe I wanted to. For most of the previous decade, I had been funding my new business investments off a significant margin line with a Canadian chartered bank. The line was secured by my extensive portfolio of publicly traded securities or stocks. When the value of all publicly traded stocks plummeted in the fall of 2008, my available credit at the bank also plummeted. Had I not sold one significant energy stock-holding late that summer, my margin calls would have been painful and embarrassing. (As an aside, the energy company whose shares I sold went bankrupt a few months later. I am still beholden to the contrarian trader—David Fenwick—who talked me into liquidating that position.)

The bottom line—almost half of my total worth simply disappeared over the course of a few short months in the fall of 2008. It was a humbling experience. The destruction of value in my wealth meant the entire value gained from the work I had done over the previous five-plus years had been lost in a few short months. Evaporated. Kaput. Gone. Before you reach for the Kleenex, I do realize that for many people the economic hardship was far worse—far more challenging—as leverage had literally destroyed their savings.

As citizens of the western world scrambled to get their financial houses in order, we watched governments desperately prop up poorly managed companies that would have gone under or been bought out in any other climate. The goal was to save the economy and thus all of mankind. (Okay, forgive the sarcasm, but my somewhat acerbic Dragons' Den partner, Kevin O'Leary, openly advocated "letting the big dogs die," suggesting that the free market had spoken and we were culling out inefficient producers. For once, I totally agreed with him!) In December 2008, following the American lead, the big three Canadian automakers lined up to ask for multi-billion-dollar bailout packages. They eventually got them, a risky use of taxpayer dollars to my mind. Who were we really protecting? Two months after

President Bush's $700-billion bailout of Wall Street in late 2008, we found out that $18 billion of that money was paid out as executive bonuses. Performance bonuses? It couldn't be.... Like many people, I wondered, *What is really going on here? Are the inmates running the asylum again?*

My issue wasn't so much over the size of those bonuses as it was over the logic of paying them at all. I have spent more than twenty-five years working as an investment banker. Our firm earned relatively sizeable commissions or fees—some would say they were generous to a fault—for brokering, financing and arranging billion-dollar deals in the energy industry. But our compensation model was negotiated at arm's length, up front, and was based on performance—no deal done meant no commission earned. In this instance, it appeared that executives were now negotiating bonuses for running underperforming companies. The motivation for the compensation seemed to be a mixture of fear and greed. Corporate boards of directors feared losing the senior executives who were thought necessary to turn the faltering companies around. Many executives (but not all) appeared to take advantage of the situation to hold their own shareholders hostage and fuel their own greed. Perception is reality—and the perception of what these executive bonuses were rewarding was to me simply bad. Really bad.

"When you're investing in someone, think of it as a relationship rather than a transaction. The best relationships are based on trust, respect and mutual interests. And those relationships are the best way to make money."—WBW

I know some people believe that fear and greed rule the world, especially the business world. But the public outcry over this kind of compensation led me to believe that we as a society haven't really lost our basic commitment to human values, such as fairness and integrity. But somewhere along the way, we may have come to believe that success was worth letting go of those values, whatever the cost. I know that the cost of my early financial success was paid for by my health and by my family. For others, the cost of success was nothing less than the loss of their personal reputations. Greed and the pursuit of material wealth can be a blindfold—which is best removed by redefining success.

Winning at All Costs

After some thirty years in business I really do think I have seen it all. I have seen people misrepresent the facts, weasel out on deals, and take unfair advantage of their own partners, clients and competitors. I have seen people lose their reputation while they gain their riches. And I have seen families and friendships, including to a degree my own, almost destroyed by the overpowering pursuit of material success.

The world abounds with headline-grabbing scandals, but there are also far too many examples of bad business behaviour that don't make the front page. There are many who treat every negotiation as a battle that has to be won at all costs, rather than finding a reasonable compromise. There are those (such as a former employer of mine) who would nickel-and-dime a client (or his own staff) until nobody could walk away from the table happy. And there are people who treat every business deal as just a financial transaction, rather than an opportunity for building or continuing a longer-term relationship.

"Rather than trying to squeeze every dime out of a client or supplier, focus on making every deal a fair deal. That principle is fundamental to longer-term business success."—WBW

There is an almost legendary story of the chairman of one of the major Canadian investment banks who regularly said to his team: "If you see a competitor drowning in a pool, don't ever throw him a life jacket. Find a garden hose, run it down his throat and finish the job!" It apparently inspired his team to greater glory, but is that person someone you would ever want around your family? Someone you would ever want as a business partner? Not me.

A lot of people think this cutthroat attitude is a normal part of doing business, and, sure, some "succeed" with this ruthless approach. For them, the only thing that matters is the bottom line. "Money has no conscience" is a saying I've heard many times on the set of Dragons' Den. I've been accused of being naïve and soft to a fault. I obviously don't agree. No, it's not just about the money. I do know how to make money, a lot of money—I have proven that—but at the end of the day, your coffin doesn't care how much money you have. It is just a coffin. And if your legacy is tied to the size of your estate, and not the memories you leave behind and the impact you have made on this earth, then your life journey might have been wasted.

Developing a Moral Compass

A regular compass consistently guides geographical direction. A moral compass is a mental process that consistently points a person in a particular direction in life. A moral compass is an internal tool. Some might refer to it as a conscience or a feeling that consistently guides personal beliefs and actions.

From my experience, most people either have a strong ethical sense when they start out in business or they develop one along the way. Watching people suffer from the consequences of bad or unethical choices will eventually raise the question, Is it really worth it? And the wise ones soon discover that unethical actions or values never are worth pursuing.

For me, the lesson about sticking to a strong moral compass—with a focus on doing what's right—came when I was starting out. As I mentioned, early in my career I worked closely with someone who was sadly lacking moral standards. In fact, if it's possible for anyone to be completely devoid of ethics, he came close. He treated his employees unfairly, without respect, honesty or encouragement, and he certainly didn't deal squarely with his clients. Within a few weeks of joining his firm, I discovered that he had a willingness to share confidential information around town when it might serve his own self-interest. I realized that being associated with him was not wise, and I got out as soon as I could extricate myself from that situation. Unfortunately for me, that took almost eighteen, miserable, frustrating months.

That experience helped me get clarity about what kind of businessperson I wanted to be "when I grew up"—I wanted to be someone who is both fair and respectful, who negotiates a square deal with mutual interests in mind, who invests in people rather than projects, who follows through on promises and who delivers quality service every time. I wanted to be someone for whom a handshake creates a bond much stronger and more enduring or meaningful than a written contract. My time with my immoral colleague was influential in guiding me to my moral compass.

Thanks to my upbringing, by parents who lived by strong ethical principles, I have always enjoyed a heightened sense of or awareness of what is right or wrong. I didn't always pay attention to my moral compass in the early days of my various careers, but I actually did find it over time, and that moral compass has certainly strengthened *with* time. I've seen what happens to people who operate ethically in business and life and those who don't. Some of my own mistakes confirmed what I already knew—that the consequences of flexible or misguided moral or ethical standards are just too dire for me.

> "The most important asset you will ever have, and the one that appreciates the most, is the human capital you hire, develop and retain."—WBW

Having a strongly principled foundation is not the only way to succeed. Sure, there are those who have achieved material wealth without principles. But, to me, an honest path is a worthy path and this is the best path to success. Success is simply more sustainable and rewarding when it's achieved without jeopardizing one's integrity. You will sleep better at night. You will gain financial success without losing the respect of your employees, your customers or your competitors. More importantly to most of us, you will secure the respect of your own children, the ultimate judges of your actions and legacy.

Failures Can Lead to Success

A long-term commitment to business ethics has been foundational for my own business successes. When I was privileged to join in founding FirstEnergy Capital Corp. with three great partners back in 1993, we deliberately built the firm from scratch as an investment bank with a conscience. Today, only two decades later, that former start-up dealer is one of the global energy industry's leading investment banks, a firm that has brokered thousands of financings and merger-and-acquisition (M&A) deals totalling well over $250 billion.

By 1997, just shy of my fortieth birthday, I was named to Canada's Top 40 under 40, the Caldwell Partners' prestigious program, which celebrates accomplishment early in life. Two years later, I was listed as one of the *Globe and Mail's* somewhat influential Top 20 Deal Makers in Canada. The following year, I was again honoured by the *Globe* to be recognized as one of the Top 10 Merger and Acquisition specialists active in Canada. The lists were prepared very subjectively, but I was on them, so obviously someone out there was noticing the progress of my career and my pursuit of success.

I'm proud of my record in business, and I have enjoyed tremendous and unexpected financial success because of it. But I know that people who put themselves up on a pedestal are easy targets, and so I'm quick to admit that I've been far from perfect. I'm particularly ashamed to confess that while I focused on keeping my priorities and passion aimed at the business world, I truly failed to do right by my wife, family and friends. And I failed to look after my health.

> *"Money is important, but don't forget what makes life really worth living: family, friends and health. Success is about passion guided by priorities."—WBW*

In the process of building my various business interests through my day-to-day investment banking duties and my leadership role as chief operating officer (COO), then president and later chairman of our successful investment bank, I let my hunger and passion for material wealth and business success bring me, quite literally, to my knees. I chased deals seven days a week, every hour of the day and night. And I paid a high price. My almost twenty-year marriage was in shreds. I suffered a strained and almost distant relationship with my children. And my personal life—emotional, physical and spiritual—was completely out of balance. By mid-2001, I faced my own personal crisis: I was completing my divorce to my university sweetheart while struggling to share time with three kids, whom I sometimes felt all but resented their previously continuously absent father, and as if this wasn't challenge enough, I also was dealing with the onset of a severely advanced case of prostate cancer. Not good.

It took a series of dramatic life events to awaken me to the fact that my core values and priorities were completely messed up. It's a familiar story behind business success: *Ambitious entrepreneur sacrifices his relationships and health to make it big.* I lived that story. Part of developing my own functional moral compass, which hasn't always been easy, has been to balance my passion for business with my other life priorities. In fact, I ultimately had to reset my priorities pretty much from scratch.

If you had asked me what my definition of success was ten years ago, I would have answered "closing deals and making money," along with the traditional material rewards of such success. When the multi-faceted personal crises I faced peaked in 2001, I was forced to do some intensive work to deal with life issues, priorities and balance. Subsequently, my priorities shifted dramatically—I will explain a lot more about that process and what came of it later in this book. What I have learned the hard way is that work/life blend/balance is essential. I am still ambitious, and, yes, still focused on being successful. But my philosophy of how best to define and then achieve success has changed dramatically—by almost 180 degrees.

When my son was about twelve years old, we sat down to talk about a decision I had made to effectively give the vast majority of my personal wealth to charity—both over time and at the end of my time. He looked at me with a slightly worried expression. "But what if I'm not successful?" he asked. It was a timely opportunity to share my evolving belief with him that my definition of success was no longer focused on material possessions or artificial measures of achievement but rather it was ultimately about happiness, particularly my happiness and that of those around me. Understanding that success comes when you are happy because you have a career that's rewarding, you have good to great relationships with family and friends, and you are making a real difference in your community. All of these things now define success for me. I do understand that if you don't have enough money to cover the basic necessities of life, then the drive to attain security is compelling. But once you have enough (which is the topic of another discussion taken up later in this book), your measured wealth really doesn't define success. In fact, I would observe that wealth, fame and status become very superficial measures of real happiness.

I know what some of you are thinking—*that's easy for you to say.* But when I speak to various groups across the country, this work/life balance issue strikes the biggest chord. Signing another business deal, attending another charity auction, heading off with clients to race dune buggies in Mexico, going whitewater rafting in Ecuador or attending the Masters Golf Tournament in Augusta, Georgia, mean absolutely nothing if you're never there to tuck your children in at night. To share quality time. I know. I know all too well. In this book I will share with you my challenges.

> *"What we have done for ourselves dies with us; what we have done for others and the world remains and is immortal."—Albert Pike*

A Better Path

I believe that the path to achieving real success depends on first establishing your own functional definition of success and then forging and adjusting your priorities to allow you to pursue it. I've already explained that I have learned that success isn't about power or prestige or the size of your wallet, but rather the quality of all aspects of your health, your relationships with family and friends, being committed to lifelong learning, having a passion for what you do to make a living, and then leaving the world a little (or a lot) better than you found it. For me, life started over again with a commitment I made to myself to find a new definition of success, and then reprioritizing my life based on the things that mattered most.

"Until you have done something for humanity, you should be ashamed to die."—Horace Mann

So how can legitimate business and community leaders regain trust and re-establish credibility after the landslide of negative media coverage that many of their colleagues have so rightly been subjected to over the last decade? Part of the way we can regain that trust is by celebrating the people and the companies that are getting it right. There are many such stories. But I'll start by telling the one I know best. FirstEnergy.

Here is a man dressing for form and function. This gambler dons his vest with the same determination as a holster. It rides his shoulders like a confidant, careful with the odds, unafraid of consequences.

Compadre or alternate, its shape speaks allusion, the formal V, the sleeves insisting on the arms that furnish flex, the hands that will deal the cards.

Back to a backdrop; check to see if the suit is riding into town. Keep the game private, trust the secret location, prepare for the skirmish. Risk or chance, speculate and wager. Salto and hazard: what's in a shadow but a shadow? Only a silhouette, a contour, a profile tracing the binary between dark and light, that twilight glimmer.

Bulletproof and waist-fitting. Garment and chorister. Legalis intricarus. Tricks and perplexities.

This man will wager all and come away ahead, luck through the play to the other side. Ready or not, scan the collaborators, note the tricksters, the confidence men waiting in the wings.

Best to don some armour. The dealer is always a wastrel.

Investment.

—Aritha van Herk

Two

FirstEnergy

The iBanking Journey

I was among the first 225 graduates (yes, the first 225!) from the University of Calgary's at-that-time-only-part-time MBA program way back in 1985, and to my knowledge, I was the first to graduate with a major in entrepreneurship. Thanks to my engineering undergrad studies, I found the mathematics of finance and accounting reasonably straightforward. Thanks to earning an MBA scholarship from one of the leading Canadian investment banks, I subsequently interviewed with that firm and soon after began my roller-coaster career in investment banking.

I spent almost five years working in the corporate finance department with McLeod Young Weir (now ScotiaMcLeod or Scotia Capital) and had the great privilege of working with, and for, some of the best people in the business. James MacDonald, David Wilson, Dan Sullivan, John McCormick, Michael Grandin, Brian Porter, Rob McLelland and the late Gordon Cheeseborough and, of course, others were all important contributors to my incredible learning curve at McLeod. I recall vividly the time each one of them took to contribute to my career based on their respective experiences in the demanding but lucrative world of investment banking. Many of these mentors went on to enjoy high-profile careers of their own in the world of Canadian finance. I mention them because of the privilege I enjoyed in their mentorship.

In my time with McLeod Young Weir, I was constantly pushing the team in Calgary to focus *only* on the energy industry, and let other business sectors in the West be covered by our specialist teams out of Toronto, but internal politics prevented that from happening. After almost five years I left to work in a boutique firm that was indeed focused on energy. Somewhat amusingly, almost three months after I left the firm, McLeod's internal newsletter acknowledged my fifth anniversary with the firm—apparently no one noticed I was gone (except the payroll department).

My time at the boutique advisory firm I joined after leaving McLeod remains the darkest and most difficult chapter in my life. After the first week, it was almost eighteen months of living hell. I have shared already my experience with my unethical colleague at the firm. I still had much to learn. The other members of the staff and I were always in a defensive position, walking on eggshells whenever the boss was around. He was a corporate bully and used his power to abuse his team constantly. The employee turnover was high for obvious reasons. Basically I now manage my business ventures to run in a manner almost the opposite of how he would have run them. Respect for and loyalty to my staff, and honesty in dealings with clients, suppliers and even competitors are all important to me. Parting ways with that boutique advisory firm was inevitable given the clear disconnect between our respective morals and values. But getting out wasn't as easy as just quitting, given that I was working on commission, had brought in significant business and needed to wait for a few deals to close.

> *"Be respectful and fair in your business relationships. I treat people I invest in as equal partners: success happens when everyone pays attention to the mutual interests of the partners."—WBW*

As an aside: there is a common perception that entrepreneurs are born risk-takers. When I studied entrepreneurship at the University of Calgary, risk and risk-taking were prevalent themes, but I came to believe that entrepreneurs are *not* risk-takers for the sake of taking risks, like gamblers chasing the adrenaline rush of rolling the dice in Las Vegas, but rather, I firmly believe that entrepreneurs simply view risk differently. Yes, they may have a higher threshold for risk tolerance than others—but they don't take risks for the thrill of it. Rather, true entrepreneurs genuinely believe that they can and will succeed in the business adventure at hand. That said, I found myself miserable. I was caught in an unhealthy work environment, but I was still unwilling to take the risk of starting out in business on my own—until a brief conversation that took the apparent risks away. Or was it just my perception of the apparent risks that changed?

I was on a flight with John Halliwell, an executive of my employer's top client. It was mid-1991 and we were off to Toronto to see if we could interest institutional fund managers in investing directly in mature oil and gas properties rather than just in oil and gas exploration and production companies. (This was an idea of mine that was simply five years ahead of its time. The subsequent growth of that sector proved that my thesis was correct.) On the flight, John asked me if the guy I was working for really had what it would take to grow his advisory firm into a full-service investment bank. Thinking *"never,"* I hesitated, knowing that I was talking to my employer's most important client. John said, "From your pause, I think I know the answer." He went on to say, "I just wanted to share that if you were ever to go out on your own, I would hire you." It might not have appeared to be much of an endorsement to some, but to me, at that moment, it was all the encouragement I needed. John had just taken away all the risk—in my mind—of starting a new investment bank. Although John ended up not directing any work my way for several years, I still credit him with encouraging the decision to move forward and start out on my own. The fact that he would hire me gave me confidence that others, too, would employ my services. That conversation set in action a course of events that would be pivotal in my life—and in my role as a co-founder of one of Canada's premier investment banks.

Wilson Mackie & Company, Inc.

My first significant entrepreneurial venture was a small investment-banking advisory-services firm we called Wilson Mackie & Company, Inc. Our focus was brokering oil and gas properties and small companies. Jamie Mackie was my first business partner. While Jamie had absolutely no prior experience in investment banking or in brokering oil and gas properties, he had honesty and integrity, two of the most important factors that make a great partner. He also really understood the metrics of value in all aspects of the energy industry. With Jamie, a handshake was all you ever needed to move forward. He benefitted from relevant education, having graduated with a master's degree in resource management from Yale University, and was very well connected, having grown up in Calgary as part of a respected, long-time Alberta family, and having worked "downtown" in the energy industry for more than a decade.

A month after starting Wilson Mackie, I vividly remember stopping to visit a client of my former firm, a wealthy energy and real-estate investor located in Toronto, to apologize for leaving my prior firm, and for the fact that I could no longer work for him in searching out acquisition opportunities. He said, "I want to hire you again." I instantly balked, knowing that I could not solicit former clients, and advised him that I could not work for him. He interrupted me and said, "Look, I am a lawyer, I understand the law, you are clearly *not* soliciting my business, but I am clearly telling you that I want to hire you. Now can we get a relationship papered?" Frankly, this was the pivotal moment in Wilson Mackie's growth. We set up a retainer-based relationship, with a commission structure that was fair in the event of success, and with this client, our running overhead was covered. (Postscript: we ended up helping with several acquisitions, which turned enormous profits for our client, and appropriately delightful commissions for Wilson Mackie. His faith in us was well rewarded—a true win-win result. And I extend my appreciation to him—he knows who he is!)

Together, Jamie and I built Wilson Mackie into a significant business in the course of two short years. Jamie was well known and well liked. His ability to open doors was unrivalled in my experience. I would sometimes phone an oil company four or five times trying unsuccessfully to get a senior-level meeting and Jamie would say, "Let me try." An hour later he would tell me: "We're on for three o'clock on Friday."

"Don't be afraid to try something new. Take a few risks, make a few mistakes. That's how you will learn. I've made money on many deals because of the mistakes I've made on earlier deals."—WBW

Wilson Mackie's ten-or-so employees ultimately formed the core of the corporate finance group for FirstEnergy when we formed that firm in the fall of 1993. Jamie and I continued as business partners for another seven years before he left to start another of the very successful investment banks in Calgary, J.F. Mackie & Co., which itself has been merged into another entity, and Jamie has moved on yet again, building on success each time. I remain very grateful for his key role in helping build two successful—and ethically grounded—businesses.

FirstEnergy Capital Corp.

By the time I was involved in co-founding FirstEnergy, I had a very clear idea of the kind of business I wanted to help build next. FirstEnergy was the brainchild of four oil patch mavericks who intended to create a unique, full-service, specialty investment banking boutique focused exclusively in energy. The co-founders were Murray Edwards, a good friend and an accomplished lawyer-turned-merchant banker, whom I had met through student politics at the University of Saskatchewan, as well as Rick Grafton and Jim Davidson, two of the very best institutional equity salesmen in the country—each working with boutique-style investment banks in Calgary—both of whom I got to know through my years in corporate finance. It took us almost nine months to plan what the firm would look like, meeting every second Tuesday evening at Calgary's downtown Petroleum Club. We carefully choreographed our movements in and out of the "Pete Club," always arriving and leaving separately, so that no one in the tightly knit Calgary business community would take notice of our clandestine meetings and wonder what we were up to.

Rick, Murray, Jim and I enjoyed one another's unique and often complementary but very different talents. Our differences truly made us stronger as a team.

There is no doubt that Murray Edwards will go down as one of the greatest entrepreneurs in Canadian history. His long-term impact on the Canadian economy is only beginning to be appreciated, and the rest of the world has only begun to sense what he is capable of achieving through the enterprises he has often built from scratch. Simply put, he has created work for tens of thousands of Canadians. Untold billions of dollars have been generated for those who stepped into the Murray companies as they evolved and grew. Murray has always been driven, even back in university when he was completing a four-year commerce degree in only three years while, at the same time, participating in high-level student politics. He went on to study law in Toronto. He would often call me at midnight, Alberta time, just after he had finished doing his homework, to talk about life, the stock market and the economy. He was at the time the youngest person ever made a partner at the leading law firm of Burnet Duckworth & Palmer. Soon after achieving that status, he chose to leave the practice of law and become a merchant banker under his own name, operating as Edco Financial Holdings Ltd. Murray has enjoyed more significant

"Every good partnership has to be built on trust. I tend to see people as trustworthy until they prove me wrong. I am okay with a few mistakes."—WBW

independent business successes than anyone I can think of. He is brilliant in terms of strategy, tactics, acquisition and execution. He is not afraid of failure or mistakes, instead calling them all "challenges" to learn from. He brought vision, organization and discipline to the FirstEnergy partners' table, playing a key role in helping to turn a fledgling brokerage house into what would become one of the energy industry's leading investment banks.

Clients and competitors would often observe—enviously—that Rick Grafton was the type of salesman who could create enough wind to make a turkey fly on a calm day. He would get so excited or passionate about what he was selling that you couldn't help but give him an order! In an upward-trending market, he was one of the best salesmen in any sector anywhere. Rick was extremely well connected to numerous institutional investors and to a number of energy company management teams, relationships that proved invaluable to our firm. Rick was instrumental in bringing in new clients. These were clients with whom we formed what we fondly referred to as "cradle-to-grave" relationships: we would participate in their initial financings and the resulting initial public offerings, continue to nurture the relationship during the growth phase, and advise on the final exit strategy—sometimes only a few years later. Rick left FirstEnergy in the early 2000s to set out on his own and has enjoyed success in almost every venture he has put his enviable passion into.

In good times and in bad times, i.e., the volatile stock markets we live with, Jim Davidson is one of the best salesmen this country has ever seen. He is focused, dedicated and driven. His selling skills are constantly refined on the golf courses, in hockey arenas and in the boardrooms of our institutional and corporate clients. I still remember a partner in a financing deal we were doing for Rio Alto Exploration Ltd. advising us that one of Rio Alto's largest shareholders was upset with the financing we were co-leading. He said they were planning to sell their entire position into our just-announced "bought-deal" financing, a trading decision that would disrupt the market and undermine the entire deal. Jim picked up the phone: the Rio Alto financing hung awaiting the result. Almost an hour later, Jim got off the phone with the client, smiled, threw his hands in the air, and advised us that he had not only convinced the client not to sell, but that the client was now a lead order in the financing in front of us. "Inconceivable!" as was said in the classic movie *The Princess Bride* so many times, but he had saved the $100-million financing from ruin. Jim is currently the chairman and CEO of FirstEnergy, and he uniquely deserves both titles.

Both Jim and Rick were unique in the investment industry because they had extraordinary relationships both with corporate issuers *and* with institutional investors. Most salesmen only knew the investors. Most corporate-finance guys only knew the issuers. But Rick and Jim were powerful crossovers: they understood both perspectives because they spent time on both sides—and enjoyed deep relationships wherever they roamed. They were really classic entrepreneurs—capable of navigating circles around our competitors—who often didn't even see them coming.

Why was I there? I wondered that at times! I think I brought the ability to multitask at a very high level—what one friend would call "juggling chainsaws while blindfolded." As COO, then president, and eventually chairman, I was responsible for keeping the thousand-and-one things that needed to be done from day to day from falling through the cracks. While I was strong in finance, my real gift and passion was—and is—marketing, so I often took the lead in creating the marketing strategies that would help FirstEnergy stand out from the crowd and outrun the old boys, meaning primarily the monolithic and bureaucratic bank-owned dealers. Our investor conferences were world-class, our commitment to community unrivalled, our broad cross-section of client events the envy of our competitors. On top of my management role, I also worked full-time as a senior partner in the corporate finance group with a particular emphasis on merger-and-acquisition transactions, for which I had a passion.

After all, I had to carry my weight there to earn my share of the deal-origination fees, fees that were often a significant part of the senior partners' compensation package.

The balance of our team, when we opened, was the result of a carefully orchestrated street sweep designed to gather the best of the best—people the founding partners judged would fit the chemistry and share the vision of a full-service, energy-focused investment bank. The first obvious team member was my own partner, Jamie Mackie. In addition, Rick Grafton was aware that Dean Prodan and Donna LeBoeuf were frustrated at the venerable local investment bank Peters & Co. Limited and could be, and were, talked into joining. Jim Davidson knew that a young up-and-coming analyst would want to work with him, and the highly intuitive Scott Inglis did, indeed, come over after four hours of deliberation, followed soon after by Rafi Tahmazian—both from First Marathon. Our second analyst (being very analytical) was also identified on day one, but it took us almost a year of negotiation to recruit Martin Molyneaux, who has since been consistently ranked among Canada's top research analysts. Sheila Kaiser joined me early in the planning of FirstEnergy. I say *me* because the other partners' identities were kept a secret until regulatory approvals were received and they could quit their jobs. Sheila joined on the public pretense of starting an oil company, so that no one in downtown Calgary would know that an investment bank was being formed. Last but not least, we convinced Mark Phipps to take a leap of faith from a bank-owned dealer to head of corporate finance at FirstEnergy, and with his appointment, the starting lineup was complete. Actually not quite complete: how could I forget Wiley Auch, our first chief financial officer? He was the only interviewee who said he wanted to be the best CFO an investment bank ever had,

> *"No one comes to the table with everything needed to build a successful business. Often the most successful people are the ones who've built a team of partners to help them along."—WBW*

and that was the standard to which he worked every day after joining us in the first week of business!

With the four founders and the incredible team we had assembled, we believed that as long as we all played our respective roles to our respective strengths, we would have something in FirstEnergy that would make us a pretty powerful competitor. Future developments ultimately proved our intuition right.

Partners in a successful enterprise have to share a common vision, and we certainly did. Our vision was to create an investment bank with a conscience. Just as people are susceptible to moral failures, so are companies. Breaking basic rules of good business can ruin a great company. And so, in a very real sense, we built integrity into our business plan. We didn't just want to be big—we wanted to be good. Very good. Being professional, effective and profitable wasn't enough. We set out from day one to maintain the highest standards of integrity in all our dealings with one another, with staff, with clients and with competitors. Not only did this commitment to ethics reflect our individual personal values, we also knew that it would be a powerful marketing differentiator in an industry known for the legendary (and thankfully mainly mythical) Gordon Gekko mantra from the movie *Wall Street*: "greed is good." A phrase that reflects a pathetic perspective on life, I would now argue. The three key elements of FirstEnergy's Mission Statement—which was developed by the senior management team through a long and heated debate over every single word—truly set the firm apart from its peers: "We take an aggressive, innovative, insightful and creative approach to relationships and to the business; an unrivalled commitment to clients, community and excellence; and a promise to maintain the highest level of integrity in all our dealings." This Mission Statement, created in the early 1990s,

> *"When we built FirstEnergy, we didn't just plan what we would do, we also planned who would do what. We built the firm based on the strengths of each of the key partners."—WBW*

still resonates today. I am proud of my contribution to that statement and to the firm that lives by it.

Relationships First

Our primary goal was to create an investment bank capable of cradle-to-grave relationships and service. We wanted to begin our relationships with companies when they started up, and we wanted to be their dealer of choice when it was time for them to sell, whether that was five years or twenty-five years later. As the companies we backed in their infancy matured and grew, we never wanted to lose the relationship to a larger investment bank. Many investment banks—even today—are primarily concerned with the current transaction: the deal in front of them. We were on the other extreme: a heavily relationship-driven investment bank. Our business model was based on really knowing our clients and their business. That included firm-to-firm relationships, as well as person-to-person relationships, so it wasn't just the senior people who understood the clients—it was people at all levels. We also focused on treating the service and support firms and their people, the accountants and the lawyers and so forth who worked on deals with us, with more than just respect—we valued our relationships of all kinds. Paying suppliers quickly and offering loyalty to those that were good to us when we started were a given.

Our relational approach to business meant that we took a long-term view of every transaction. Rather than trying to squeeze every dime out of a client or supplier, we focused on making every deal a square deal, one that would keep our clients or suppliers and partners coming back to the table to do business with us. This principle was fundamental to our success as a firm. And often it was our point of difference with our competitors, whether they were small or large.

Our commitment to fair dealing was beautifully demonstrated in 2005, when FirstEnergy established a strategic partnership with Société Générale (SocGen), one of the world's biggest and most innovative banks. This relationship was incredibly significant for

FirstEnergy because it allowed us to effectively extend our reach around the globe. The partnership also gave Canadian energy companies access to new sources of debt-based financing, which was important because debt financing had become choked by the traditionally risk-averse Canadian Schedule A banks. In return for bolstering our business plan, SocGen took a significant minority interest in the equity account of FirstEnergy. SocGen was wise in not wanting to buy 100 percent of the firm, knowing that the key assets of the firm rode the elevators every day, and equity ownership was a key driver in the compensation plan and resulting loyalty of the revenue-generating dealmakers.

Attracting a huge international bank as a strategic partner was a major coup. The president of SocGen Canada, Pierre Matuszewski, was a key colleague and friend of mine from a decade earlier at McLeod Young Weir, at which time he was running the Montreal office. His request in late 2004 for access to FirstEnergy's highly regarded proprietary research products was really just opening the door to the relationship that we eventually built firm-to-firm. Early meetings in New York showed the senior partners at FirstEnergy that we shared many values: SocGen truly understood and respected our Mission Statement. SocGen was a global leader with an outstanding product offering and valuable global perspective. They chose to do business with FirstEnergy over other investment banks because they were attracted by our knowledge, depth, ethics and drive. And by the partners who were the engine of growth at FirstEnergy.

There is an old saying in the deal world that you know you've got a good business deal when both sides walk away equally unhappy. Well, we proved that's not always the case. At the closing function to celebrate our partnership, both sides of the negotiation were clearly happy. Both sides thought they had accomplished a good-to-great deal. Which means each of us could have given a bit more, or taken a bit more. We knew we had done something right because we ended up with a strong, mutually rewarding relationship based on fundamental respect for each other's values. FirstEnergy negotiated deal terms that were compellingly advantageous in economic terms both for us and for SocGen. Neither side had to lose anything. It was the cliché win-win deal.

Gold Is in the Details

In addition to pursuing a relationship-based approach to client business, the second pillar of our firm was to focus on the highest ethical standards in all of our dealings, both internally and externally. Some investment dealers only think about sales and trading, research and corporate finance when they describe their business. The one area that is routinely ignored or overlooked, because of its reputation for being just a necessary evil, is the back-office function. That area includes all the non-revenue-generating functions that are essential to the firm, but don't appear to contribute directly to the bottom line—basically office administration, internal finance, human resources and regulatory compliance.

> *"I agree with this quote: 'If you have integrity, nothing else matters. If you don't have integrity, nothing else matters.'"—WBW*

At FirstEnergy, we never considered compliance a necessary evil at any level. It was frustrating at times, but critical to our reputation. Since commencing operations in 1993, FirstEnergy has enjoyed an unparalleled and enviable compliance record, initially under the leadership of Wiley Auch. We are incredibly proud of what we understand to be a nearly unique record as one of a few, if not the only, firm in Canada that has never even been fined or had its wrist slapped for even minor regulatory infractions—and those infractions are often minor and innocent, based on processes slipping, and very common in the industry. We understood and respected both the letter and the spirit of the law, and this led us to develop systems and attract people who would uphold our standards. We also enjoyed a very upfront and respectful relationship with the regulatory agencies that governed every aspect of our business.

What we did right was to empower people to invest a higher level of attention to detail, use their best discretion, and always err on the side of doing things right. If we ever fell into a grey zone and earned a regulatory warning, we were always forthcoming about our error, and would make the required corrections immediately and without debate.

Putting such an emphasis on regulatory compliance cost us money in additional overhead. We probably spent more money and attention on compliance and financial reporting than most of our competitors would think reasonable. We moved more slowly in some situations than our competitors did because we wanted to make sure our *i*'s were all dotted and the *t*'s were properly crossed. But to us, it was well worth it. It was an investment in the highest level of ethical behaviour, which was just good business in every measure.

An Investment Bank with a Heart

The thing that really made us an investment bank with a conscience was our unrivalled focus on community investment. From day one, we decided to give 2.5 percent of pre-tax profits to charity.

FirstEnergy's commitment to giving back to the community appeared to be in sharp contrast to the giving levels of the rest of corporate Canada. Around that time, fewer than 3 percent of Canadian businesses claimed any charitable donations at all; on average they were donating less than 1 percent of pre-tax profits. We wanted to do more. A lot more. For many good reasons.

"FirstEnergy didn't set out to be a leader in corporate philanthropy. We did set out to be a leader in investment banking. And we used charitable giving as a marketing tool."—WBW

We immediately set out to be proactive philanthropists. Since inception in 1993, FirstEnergy and its partners have donated tens of millions of dollars to more than three hundred different charities and community organizations. These donations and the causes that then benefitted have touched the lives of countless thousands.

The 2.5 percent threshold is actually our *minimum* standard. The firm often significantly exceeds this amount. The 2.5 percent calculation doesn't include individual partner contributions or money raised during client relationship events. FirstEnergy has a reputation for throwing some of the best parties in the city, and these popular events have helped us to engage others in the community to give back through the FirstEnergy Community Foundation, which has also raised or generated many more millions for charity.

Today, FirstEnergy is widely regarded as one of Canada's leading socially responsible companies and is often held up as a model for other corporate citizens, and not just in the world of finance. Its commitment to community has been a core building block—key to FirstEnergy's overall success. The real testament to the philanthropic trail we blazed is the overwhelming influence FirstEnergy has had on corporate Calgary's social conscience.

Here is a man who yearns to be Icarus.

Despite hubris, the heat of the sun melting the wax fashioning the wings and so precipitating his fabled fall, its mythological portal to fire and ambition. Straight into story and cautionary tale and the rumour of desire.

Entranced by the kernel of flight, leaving earth, lifting away from the pull of gravitation's weight and orbit. Flight, that magic exodus, freedom from hand to yonder. The replica bird, to scale or beyond, wings aching for release and the sky racing to catch glide.

Light and sky a portal to intention and yearning, slipping earth's surly bonds for vaults of azure.

Industrial between the gunmetal compromise of buildings, the sky shrunk to mere wedge, constricting light, heat, the reverie of clouds. And from this tunnel, ironclad industrial structure, the heavens signal a meta-dream of lucid dreaming.

Freed flight, the fantasy of weightlessness. In flight we dream, in dreams we fly.

With lucid dreaming we fly and know that we are dreaming flight, can control the flying, the dream, the soar and swoop, the hover and the climb. Lucid dreaming bestows the grace of power in the dance, the trance, the aspiration.

The man on the ground, yearning to touch the weightless sky, would fly, would top all heights, those lines of flight that come together in an arc of angles.

How to package the sky? Hold up the magic of air, the burst of light that ladders down to earth.

—Aritha van Herk

Three

Making Choices

It might seem a funny place to find inspiration, but I often quote a line from the book *Harry Potter and the Chamber of Secrets*. Going against all the school rules, Harry and his friend Ron had crawled into the cave (or chamber) beneath the girls' washroom to confront Lord Voldemort and the evil dragon-like snake. After they killed the cave-dwelling monster and basically saved the world, Dumbledore, the school's headmaster, summoned the boys to his tower office high in the castle. What he tells them as he admonishes them for breaking the very clear rules about not going into the underground lair, albeit for the right reasons, has always connected with me: "Men are not known by their abilities, but rather by their choices." He was acknowledging that they had chosen wisely in breaking the rules and, as a result, had become heroes to the school and to the world.

I've come to realize that happiness is a choice. Leaving the world a better place is a choice. As my mom used to say at dinnertime, "You have two menu choices tonight—you can take it or leave it." We may have no control over what cards we are dealt, but we do get to choose how to play the hand. In my life, with the benefit of hindsight, of course, it is clear that I've made some incredibly good choices, and some incredibly not-so-good choices.

I was fortunate to have two great role models who showed me a lot about making choices aligned with life priorities—my parents. My father, Bill Wilson, is a classic prairie gentleman. He is a man who deeply believes that his word is his bond and that a handshake seals a deal. I never had to wonder where he stood on giving back to his community as I watched him slip on his jacket after a long day at work, and head out to go door to door to help raise money for the United Way or other causes. If a stranger were stranded with a flat tire, he was the guy who would pull over first to lend a hand and see him safely on his way. I was once with my dad when he backed up on a muddy rural side road for a quarter of a mile or more so that we could then follow someone down another side road. Dad had noticed, in his rear-view mirror, that a neighbour lady had turned to drive down the side road—which was really in bad shape—and we followed her knowing that she might get stuck and need help. His moral compass for caring choices was unwavering.

My mother was equally an inspiration to me. When a fund-raiser was held for the latest local cause, there was never a question that Doreen Wilson was going to participate. I smile remembering the day she agreed to swim laps in our local pool for charity, a remarkable undertaking, given that she really was challenged in the water. Every one of her sponsors knew she couldn't swim very well, so they smugly agreed to

> *"I don't care what your choices are, I care that you've made choices and haven't just been watching from the sidelines."—WBW*

give her a dollar per lap (which in 1970 was almost the minimum hourly wage!), figuring she wouldn't be able to complete more than a few laps. She surprised everyone when she showed up at the pool with a life jacket and went on to swim forty laps doing the elementary backstroke! As a social worker, she was always doing what she could to help out the community, from coaching foster parents late at night to teaching parenting classes to new parents in the evenings. For my mom, caring for others was a key part of her moral compass.

Influencing Others

I am fortunate to have fabulous influences in my life. In addition to my parents, I had great teachers and other powerful mentors. I worked or played in different ways with each of these people or families, but each influenced me in very positive ways. I was inspired by tremendous entrepreneurial dynasties, such as the Shaw and Riddell families in Calgary, whose passion and business know-how have only increased over the succeeding generations. People such as the inimitable Allan Markin, the tireless Dick Haskayne, or the already legendary Bill Siebens, who all really walked the talk are changing the world. Scores of community organizations have benefitted from the time and passion of outstanding community leaders such as Brian and Stephanie Felesky, or any of the extraordinarily community-minded owners of the NHL hockey team, the Calgary Flames. Inspired by these leaders and many others, I have attempted to follow in their footsteps and be someone our next generation—including my children—can recognize, respect and remember as a model citizen.

Being a great role model doesn't necessarily mean your kids will follow your lead. But ultimately your children will judge your actions. So think hard about what you're doing. Do your actions inspire others? Do they motivate your children? These questions have been a huge source of personal motivation for me. I make many of my life choices based on how inspiring—or uninspiring—they will ultimately be to my children as they mature and understand the sometimes strange decisions of adults!

As my children were growing up, their mother bore the vast majority of parenting duties. Pamela did a very good job of keeping our kids humble and developing their moral compass. She kept them grounded, teaching them the value of time and money. A lot of parents dictate and instruct rather than coach. But I believe you have to let your children choose whether or not to follow your path. Pam did that. She encouraged them to make good choices, but never forced the point. She truly gave them roots based in strong prairie values. In contrast, with my flair for adventure and helping community causes in a very open and proactive way, some would observe that I gave my children wings to show them what's available to each of them in the outside world. Today my children are truly following their individual passions in endeavours ranging from education, sports, travel and community involvement to positive healthy relationships.

My oldest daughter is pursuing her passion for health and education by doing graduate and postgraduate studies in behavioural sciences while travelling the world and entering a few triathlons along the way. My youngest daughter, after graduating with an engineering degree, crossed the Atlantic Ocean working as a chef on a small sailing vessel. She then toiled for several seasons as a sailor and is now heading to culinary school after extended trekking in South America. My son has been engaged in university-level athletics and studying his undergrad program, planning for graduate studies in due course—while travelling more of the world. They are each following their own moral compass and passions, making choices and bearing the consequences of those choices. As they should be.

Shortly after separating from my wife in the summer of 1999, I talked/begged my way into a sold-out parenting course, which featured the people that wrote the parenting books so many parents rely on as the key instructors. I was surprised to be the only single parent on the course, but I figured I had some catching-up to do. One of the most memorable moments for me was the revelation when one instructor suggested that whenever

> *"I make many of my choices based on how inspiring—or uninspiring—the decisions will be to my children."—WBW*

you say to a child (or an employee), "I am proud of you," for whatever reason, you effectively take ownership of that person and their actions. If you twist the words ever so slightly and consider saying instead, "*You* must be very proud of how well *you* did," you might enjoy the smile and response you get. This statement acknowledges your connection to the outcome, but leaves them owning 100 percent of their success. Children need to walk without being pushed. I really do believe each of my children, who are now young adults, have every right to be proud of themselves for the choices they are making.

Be Consistent

Unfortunately, some of the principles I applied at the office didn't find their way home a decade or two ago. It took a dramatic wake-up call for me to realize that my commitment to treating others with respect didn't always apply—as it should have—in my personal life.

There was a time (and I'm not proud of this statement) when I thought of minding my own children for an afternoon or evening as babysitting—an unwanted chore. I always worked six-and-a-half days a week, with a practice of giving my family half a day on weekends only. One evening, I reluctantly agreed to babysit so that my wife could take care of another obligation.

I was extremely bitter about having to be home that evening. There was an art auction going on, and there was a specific item I badly wanted to own. It was a piece of art I couldn't imagine living without, an object I believed would definitely complete my world. In hindsight, this is ludicrous, even laughable—I can't even recall what the piece looked like, let alone any details that could have made it significant. But at the time, I viewed my life through an entirely different lens.

This particular evening I sulked while working in my home office. I had arranged for a designate to call me when the bidding started at the auction, which would allow me to bid for the artwork over the phone. The phone rang several times that evening, and it was always answered quickly, but not once did one of the children come to get me. I assumed the phone calls were from their friends. Eventually, the time had come and gone for the auction and I was worried, so I placed a call to the auctioneer's assistant who immediately apologized, saying, "Brett, I called your house several times. Each time a little girl told me you weren't home, and I'm sorry to tell you the piece went to another buyer."

At these words, I became infuriated. I don't ever recall being so angry. I stormed out of my office, down the long hallway, and by the time I reached my daughter's bedroom I think I had grown horns. I burst through her door and found her lying on her bed doing homework. I berated her with such ferocity that she looked up at me with wide eyes and then took shelter under her bed.

I would never have hit her, but she didn't know that at the time. She was scared and I didn't let up. I continued to demand to know why she had told the woman on the phone that I wasn't home, when I was actually in my office down the hall. I was enraged and I wasn't leaving until I got an answer. At last a little whisper came from under the bed: "Because you never are home."

Those words still ring in my ears when I recall that evening. I felt as if I had been sucker-punched by that little sentence. I realized that I had become someone whom I didn't know. Even worse, I would become someone my kids didn't know. I returned to my office in a very emotional state. Something needed to change. I turned to an online network of business friends I knew through the Young Presidents' Organization (YPO) for advice on options. I needed help. A short time after this incident, I checked myself into The Meadows, a trauma and addiction treatment centre in Wickenburg, Arizona, to deal with a number of issues, including my apparent addiction to work. Now, after years of effort, I have built quality relationships with each of my children, but only after rethinking my life's priorities.

What's on Your Gravestone?

I am proud of many of the choices I have made professionally, my choice of partners, careers or investments: they've certainly brought me to a high level of business success. And I am proud of many of the choices I have made in my personal life. I try to live with few regrets. But I do truly regret my descent into workaholism. The reasons I got there are complicated, but it was the result of the choices

I made. The consequences of those choices were very expensive. While I battled prostate cancer, I was also recovering from the end of a twenty-year marriage, and inadequate relationships with my three children who were then only eight, eleven and fourteen. Depression? Yes, that too. While there were friends everywhere I went, it was an incredibly lonely time in my life. Faced with my own mortality, and an unacceptable family environment, I did some serious and long-overdue self-assessment.

Around that time, I had the opportunity to consider a powerful question that helped me completely reprioritize my life. The question, which came from an exercise that was given to me as a member of a small group of my colleagues in YPO, went something like this: "When you pass away, what would you like people to say at your funeral? When each of your friends, family members, business partners and neighbours stands up, what will they say about you? What would the inscription on your gravestone say?"

I set about responding to this exercise with typical passion—focusing on what I wanted the outside world to acknowledge about my success as a businessman and as a philanthropist. It read well, I thought. Then the hammer dropped. The moderator of my group modified the exercise very carefully. He asked, "What exactly would your children have to say if they wrote your epitaph?" The fog suddenly lifted and I was jolted into another frame of mind. I knew what I would have *liked* them to say—that I was a great father. But I was honest enough to realize that what they would *probably* say is that I was a great businessman. That exercise was like a bucket of cold water in my face. It forced me to confront the brutally unpleasant reality that who I wanted to be was not who I really was. I have always wanted to be successful, to someday be

> "Any fool can criticize, condemn and complain, and most fools do. But it takes character and self control to be understanding and forgiving."
> —Dale Carnegie

known as a philanthropist, a leader and a businessman. But there are only so many words that can go on a gravestone, and I knew my life focus had to be consistent with my new set of priorities: to be a great father, husband and friend. My eyes were opened to a harsh new insight: I was failing in the one area of life that was truly important.

Resetting Priorities

My time at The Meadows was incredible in terms of emotion and introspection. I came to really understand that happiness is a choice, that I truly deserved to be happy and that the journey of life depended on my taking the next small step. The simple outcome was that I decided to develop a list of the top priorities for my life. The list below very clearly guides how I now spend my time, energy and money. And with it I share a few stories from my journey:

"Each of you is perfect the way you are ... and you can use a little improvement."—Shunryu Suzuki

1. Personal Health: Emotional, Physical, Intellectual

I put all aspects of my health at the top of my priority list because I have come to understand my health is my greatest asset. Without your health, not much else really matters, does it? The setting and maintaining of priorities is a personal choice; I am sharing mine to inspire others to reconsider theirs.

As a workaholic, I had let my health slip on every level: emotionally, mentally and physically. I had gone from being a highly competitive (and successful) Masters swimmer in my late twenties to gaining close to forty pounds (about eighteen kilograms) over a ten-year period. I now realize that I was severely depressed. There is no question in my mind that the physical and emotional stress I was going through as my marriage was coming to an end and as I competed in the high-paced world of investment banking opened my body up for attack from disease. I am quite certain that stress is either an accelerant or a trigger for serious health issues like cancer.

The story of my cancer journey is worth sharing, I believe, because it can serve as a warning signal to the millions of driven people—both men and women—who put their health last or next to last on their priority list. As I once heard someone say, "If you don't make time for health, eventually you'll have to make more time for illness." And that's what happened to me.

Around the time I turned forty, I had lost most of the weight I had put on in the previous decade and was back to exercising regularly—I even celebrated my fortieth birthday by running a half-marathon—largely inspired by a great friend and business partner, Ken Rowan. The primary motivation for running and losing the weight came from another friend from the YPO world. "Brett, I don't know what's going on with your health, but I'm not impressed with your weight. Have you looked in a mirror lately?" Tony Dilawri shared his observations bluntly in a call he made just to deliver a tough message. It wasn't easy to hear, but Tony was the only person who called me out, as a friend, about my bulging waistline. He might not know it, but Tony's call was a turning point in my health journey.

Around that time, I began a series of visits to high-end executive health programs, including the Mayo Health Clinic in Scottsdale, Arizona, the Scripps Institute in San Diego, California, and the Cooper Clinic in Dallas, Texas, for intense physical checkups every year or two. The discipline of regular checkups saved my life. When I was forty, a simple blood test showed my PSA level was almost zero. PSA stands for *prostate-specific antigen,* a protein produced by cells of the prostate gland which can be an indicator of cancer in the gland, or of other issues.

A month before my forty-fourth birthday, at a visit to Scripps, we discovered my PSA had climbed to 7.3 (well above the conventionally accepted benchmark for concern of 4.0). Given both the rapid increase in my PSA and the overall level, my doctor called for an immediate biopsy to be done.

It was already a tough week for me. My wife and I were finalizing the details of the divorce. On June 28, 2001, at 11 A.M., I took a call from my divorce lawyer: I was officially single again; the last couple of issues in the paperwork had been resolved amicably. At exactly 12:08 P.M.—I remember it very clearly—I received a second phone call, this time from my urologist.

"Health is at the top of my priority list because I see it as my biggest asset. Without it, nothing else matters."—WBW

He apologized that he wasn't able to deliver this news in person, as he was heading out of town for a week, but he had some troubling news to share. He told me that the biopsy had come back significantly positive (as a Gleeson 7, 4+3 for those who know the prostate cancer grading system), confirming that I had a serious case of prostate cancer. He'd taken the liberty of moving quickly to book an appointment for surgery to simply and quickly remove the prostate gland, and if I had some time, he'd like to spend a few minutes with me to explain how he thought I should handle my treatment. He reassured me that he knew what to do. However, I was reluctant to take the first opinion offered to me, and began an intense review of the alternative therapies that I was certain must exist.

To this day, I remain annoyed at the medical community's mentality about treatment options for prostate cancer. There are two primary treatment modalities: surgery or radiation. (There are other options: my advice to anyone diagnosed with prostate cancer is to explore all of them!) The specialists in each area profess to have *the* answer, and are critical of any other route to recovery. The surgery camp insists that surgery is the only bona fide solution; the radiation camp suggests radiation is the premium alternative. I discovered that both sides had a pick-me-or-you-die attitude. How is the average person supposed to decide if both sides—each one represented by highly trained professionals—argue you will die if you choose the other camp's treatment protocol?

Frustrated, I did my own research. After exploring the pros and cons of surgery versus radiation, I chose radiation. Surgery is a fine option in many cases, but in my situation, I decided that radiation was the best choice and I chose—following in the footsteps of yet another YPO friend, Denny Hop—to be treated at the Dattoli Cancer Center in Sarasota, Florida. At the time (mid-2001) this centre offered a radiation treatment program with equipment and experience that far exceeded what any facility I was aware of in Canada could offer. Today, a decade later, there are much better facilities and more options, including the same radiation treatment I selected, available to Canadians. A prime example is the recently constructed Southern Alberta Institute for Urology next to the Foothills Medical Centre in Calgary. The institute is one of the largest and most comprehensive urology centres in Canada and I was proud to be a co-lead donor on this project, along with my friend and mentor, the late and legendary Doc Seaman. As prostate cancer survivors, both Doc and I were eager to make the best possible treatment available in Alberta, so that others wouldn't have to seek treatment away from home.

Anyway, I decided that my battle with cancer was not a contest or game that I wanted to lose. I was going to win, and I needed to enlist the expertise of people who could help me beat the odds. So, in addition to conventional western medical treatment, I took the unusual step of enjoining a sports psychologist, David Pascovich from the University of Calgary, to work with me. It didn't take him long to realize I was still running very hard in my personal and business lives and he handed me a copy of *The Monk Who Sold His Ferrari* to read. This book by Robin S. Sharma is about a workaholic lawyer who breaks down, heads off to Tibet to find himself, and becomes a monk who teaches balance and inner peace. Ironically, I was "too busy" with work (I was leaving in three weeks to spend two months offline in cancer treatment after all!) to read this book about workaholism, so I handed it to a key staff member to read and work up a book report. (I relied heavily on Ruby Wallis, a colleague at FirstEnergy, to assist me in a lot of my research. As head of compliance, there is simply no one more effective than Ruby in getting to an answer.) Yes, I did fess up to my book-report shortcut when I met with David. I think it simply confirmed his suspicions!

David was an invaluable asset in my journey through cancer. It turned out he already had a personal passion for understanding the connection between attitude and long-term physical and mental health issues. He invested a lot of time with me on developing my capacity for mental toughness. The first tool that he taught me was the use of imagery or visualization, a tool I had already been taught and dabbled with successfully when I competed in numerous swimming competitions. (I was a member of relay teams that earned three bronze medals—and even broke one world record—at the World Masters Games in Toronto in 1985.) In preparation for my treatments, David helped me to visualize the cancer frying when the radiation beam was turned on. He had me imagine the *sound* of the cancer frying, and even the *smell* of the cancer frying. I then developed my own mantra that I used each morning when I was undergoing treatment: *Fry, Cry, and Die.* Did it hurt to do this? Of course not. Did it help? I am alive and very well today … I would observe it's all about attitude.

> *"In many ways, cancer was the best thing that could have happened to me because it forced me to slow down and really think about how I was living. Cancer might have saved my life."—WBW*

The second tool he gave me was to use humour and inspiration to elevate my mood, either with books or movies, or by associating with positive people. I watched the iconic sports movie *Rudy* almost every other day. *Rudy* is the story of a young man whose dream was to play football for the Fighting Irish of Notre Dame. It was an inspiring story about a young man who overcomes unbelievable odds. To this day, I am moved emotionally at the same spots in the film. For humour, I enjoyed the classic British film *Saving Grace*, an offbeat story about a housewife who turns to growing marijuana to avoid financial ruin. This is another story of triumph over adversity—but this one with hilarious twists and turns that can draw tears of laughter from the viewer.

What about consorting with positive people during my time of treatment? I was joined for a few days by a great friend, Bill Hess, then chair of the Alberta Securities Commission. He tolerated no whining or complaining (no matter how badly I golfed!). My daughters also both made the journey to Florida (my son was too young to travel alone) to spend some time with me, which was an incredible and immeasurable show of support. Also memorable was the call I took from one of my main competitors, Tom Budd, who was legendary for his ruthless (some say almost heartless) way of negotiating. I still remember and appreciate to this day his offer: "If you need a golf partner or someone to go for a run with, just give me twenty-four hours and I will be there." Having to undergo treatment almost on the other side of North America was an incredibly lonely experience for me. That offer told me more about the true character of Tom Budd than a thousand deal stories ever could.

When I was still in the process of evaluating treatment options, I had jumped on a plane to visit clinics in Florida and Nevada. A few days before departing on this relatively secret and private trip, another great YPO friend, Michael Lang, pushed me to let him join me. I assured him I was fine travelling alone, and appreciated the offer. Then, the evening I was leaving, I got a call from Milt Pahl, whose wife was also a close YPO friend, and he said, "I'm going with you to the cancer clinics. Your two choices are either I am getting on the plane in front of you, or behind you." Then he kindly laughed while he reminded me that at one time he was the welterweight boxing champion of North America. There was little doubt that he was coming with me. I will be forever grateful for the incredible support he and Michael showed me when I needed it most.

I spent most of August and September of 2001 at the Dattoli Clinic. I had chosen the 7 A.M. time slot for my radiation treatments so that I would have my entire day to exercise, read, play online (I couldn't just stop reading emails!) and to stay in touch with friends. However, by the third week, I was constantly tired: all I wanted to do each day after treatment was crawl back into bed and sleep, sometimes for twelve-plus hours each day (a big increase from the usual five to six hours I had been living on). Just after the tragedy of 9/11, I returned to Sarasota for the second phase of radiation treatment. At that time, tiny radioactive seeds, in a procedure called "brachytherapy," were surgically implanted into my prostate gland.

The recovery period on my return home was a marathon of exhaustion. I slept constantly, getting up only to eat and take medication for pain and swelling and who-knows-what-else! I was so tired that I couldn't even wake up for simple bodily functions. Given that I wasn't ready to wear Attends (adult diapers), I had a lot of laundry that first week. With time and the return of my kids every second week, I was getting up earlier to organize breakfasts and rides to school; as soon as they were off, I would fall back into bed and stay there until almost noon. I would get up again to make supper and be ready for the three kids with all sorts of questions during evening homework.

I had to contend with bladder-control issues well after treatment. Prostate cancer survivors are warned that urgency and frequency of urination are key issues in the recovery period. But until you have gone through it, it's difficult to imagine the inconvenience. I've long ago lost count of the number of times I've had to pull suddenly into a parking lot or stop beside a building and quietly urinate nearby, hoping not to be noticed. I was once crossing the U.S.–Mexico border, travelling from northern Mexico inland from Tijuana with a busload of high school students who had been house-building with my family. The washrooms in the customs building were closed for repair or cleaning, and I ran out of options. I popped around a corner—not realizing that cameras had to have been placed everywhere in the vicinity. I hadn't even finished relieving myself against a wall when a car filled with customs officers pulled up in a sliding stop. Moments later, I found myself approached by gun-toting border patrol officers before I could pull up the zipper. "Raise your hands!" took on new meaning that day. Eventually they relented and let me go—or should I say leave?

My overall treatment journey had two clear chapters: first I endured the external beam radiation treatments and related radioactive seed implants, and then, unfortunately, I had to deal with the rare and frustrating side effects of radiation. With the benefit of hindsight, I still do not regret choosing radiation as a treatment option. I do wish, however, that we'd been able to mitigate the unpleasant side effects. I know that today the protocols for managing radiation treatments and their lingering consequences are different than they were only a decade ago.

The primary side effect of my cancer journey—some five years after the initial radiation therapy—was an alarming number of severe and frequent bladder spasms combined with extensive urinary bleeding. My efforts to deal with what was a severe case of radiation cystitis could be a chapter in itself (you can find a forty-five-minute video of my health challenges in this regard on YouTube under my name). The pain of the bladder spasms was so great that I would fall over if walking, and had to pull over if driving. Because of the bleeding I was obliged to wear a catheter and leg bag for nearly four challenging months, while my medical team and I struggled to determine the exact cause of both the bleeding and the spasms while simultaneously treating the symptoms as best we could. I was hospitalized on

"As a prostate cancer 'graduate,' I have made awareness and early detection a major theme of my philanthropic work. My message is to get checked sooner rather than later. Information won't kill you, but ignorance could."–WBW

an emergency basis a total of eight times in the fall of 2007 when my catheter became plugged. I truly hope that very few people ever experience the extreme discomfort of a blocked and very full bladder. (If you are squeamish, try not to imagine using a large plastic syringe as a pump to push water into your bladder to unplug the catheter and then pump vigorously on the pump to try and removed the heavily coagulated blood from your bladder. I was successful dozens of times—but not every time.)

In addition to traditional medical options, I pursued almost every alternative form of therapy I could find. As primary treatment for radiation cystitis, I went through a total of fifty treatments of hyperbaric oxygen therapy, or HBOT (which consisted of sitting inside a small, hyperbaric chamber for two hours breathing concentrated oxygen under pressure, in the belief that literally pressing oxygen into the inside of your body would promote internal healing). From naturopaths and a Chinese herbalist to a medical intuitive and acupuncturist to work on my immune system and energy blockages, I was willing to try anything to cure this urinary system challenge. I was driven partly by frustration and partly by desperation. Although I was never suicidal, I knew I couldn't go on living with that kind of pain and dysfunction (but I wasn't anxious to just have my bladder removed and live with an external bag, as one specialist strongly encouraged me to do).

At the urging of Jasmine Hubjer, a dear friend in Toronto, I visited another intriguing healer who lived only a few blocks from me in Calgary. This gentleman explained to me, "Brett, in this world, there are unseen energies that can help you transform your illness to a place of wellness. I'm not asking you to believe in what I am doing, but I am asking you to suspend your disbelief long enough for me to work with you and for your body to heal."

Essentially he was saying, "You don't have to believe—but you can't *not* believe." With that statement I began a fascinating journey with energy, spirit guides and healing. There is no doubt in my mind that the energy work was a key part of my recovery. My radiation cystitis specialist, a urologist at the University of California, San Francisco, told me that in the month of my working with a healer he had never seen such a dramatic recovery. Was HBOT critical? Yes. Were the other conventional treatments important? Yes. Did my healer play a pivotal role in my recovery? There is no question in my mind that my healer—Hub—was key to my recovery.

As a prostate cancer survivor (although I prefer the term "graduate"), I have made disease awareness and early detection a major theme of my philanthropic work. In this arena, I am at odds with the Canadian Cancer Society. They still advise men to get their baseline PSA test and digital test at age fifty. I contracted cancer when I was forty-four. If I had followed their advice, my family would have had to exhume my body at age fifty to do the testing. Quite simply, I would have died. My message is to get checked sooner rather than later. Don't wait until fifty. In fact, don't wait at all. Start a chart of your PSA scores as soon as practical, even if you have to pay the nominal cost of the PSA testing. When it comes to health-related issues, knowledge will never kill you—ignorance just might.

In Canada, something like one in six men will develop prostate cancer, the most common cancer to affect Canadian males. Early detection is the best way to survive. If you are an adult male over thirty-five, please don't put off having a quick digital examination combined with a simple blood test that can save your life. Be a man and get it done. If you're a woman, encourage the men in your life to

"In life we all have an unspeakable secret, an irreversible regret, an unreachable dream and an unforgettable love."—Diego Marchi

get checked: make it a birthday present. And, like me, make it a priority to take care of all aspects of your health so that you can then focus on everything else that's important to you.

2. Family

After personal health comes family. The members of your family give you your core relationships and I encourage you to offer them the unconditional love and support that they would like to receive and in turn reciprocate. It isn't always possible, but it is always worth a try.

I've heard it said that the opposite of love isn't hate—it is indifference. I can't imagine indifference when it comes to family. My own struggles in my various relationships have forced me—the hard way—to make my family relationships a top priority. I learned my lesson from working late and through weekends at the office and neglecting my relationships at home. Since my divorce in the summer of 1999, my focus has been on establishing relationships with each of my kids. I say *establishing* because some days I look back and ask myself if there were ever any relationships strong enough to *re-establish*. One relationship that couldn't be mended was my relationship with my university girlfriend, my wife, Pamela. Our divorce is something I regret deeply. It wasn't just the failure of the marriage that hurt—it was the failure of our friendship. While we grew apart in terms of dreams and ambitions, she was a great partner, the mother of three wonderful children and someone for whom I still have great admiration. Her life journey has not been an easy one.

One of my favourite pastimes is travelling with my children. I have already been to almost sixty countries; most of these trips have been in the last fifteen years. I have been to more than forty of these countries accompanied by one or more of my children. I have taken trips with each child and with combinations of the kids, from sailing in the Caribbean to chasing the great apes in Uganda, and from summiting Kilimanjaro to shark-cage diving off the south coast of Africa and swimming with sea lions in the Galapagos Islands. Travelling with family is very much a priority for me: the shared experiences have created incredible parent/child bonding memories. The great benefit of travel with children who are building their own lives across North America is time to share, to talk, to plan—and to dream.

3. Friends

Friends are the essence of life. You need to seek out and support those people for whom a reciprocally rewarding relationship, either as a friend or a partner, is possible.

For many entrepreneurs, the journey can be a lonely one. When you put in a lot of hours at the office, eventually people who aren't in sync with your schedule are going to get tired of waiting. They'll leave for the banquet or barbeque without you. YPO and similar organizations such as Entrepreneurs' Organization (EO), Chief Executives Organization (CEO) and TEC Canada, to name a few, recognize that loneliness often goes with entrepreneurship and can play a critical role in helping their members build business relationships and personal friendships. YPO connects members to share ideas, pursue learning and achieve personal growth and success. Some of my best friendships have come out of that organization, among them Rich Thompson, who was responsible for getting me actively involved in the YPO world, one of the best business decisions I could have made. Rich and I have worked together closely for almost twenty years. His influence encouraged me to lift my game in many areas of life, and helped me encourage other young executives to lift theirs.

> "My new life motto is: simplify. In order to live a life of integrity—by reprioritizing, rebalancing and redefining success—sometimes you just have to get rid of the junk."—WBW

As I have said before, friends really are the essence of my life. My relationships with my friends invigorate me, protect me, excite me, teach me and encourage me. My friends have been there for me in the toughest times, and I have learned to be there for them. I am fortunate to have an extremely large network of acquaintances, with several dozen really close relationships in my inner circle.

Today, I work at being a better friend, and have developed the discipline of consistently reaching out to people. My smart phone contains a list of friends by city. When I'm travelling, I can do a better job of staying in touch with them, catching up over breakfast or lunch. I usually ask a couple of friends to join me at the same time: it gives them a chance to connect with each other, too.

There are some friends whom I don't see for a year or two, but the connection is still strong. We live our lives in separate cities, and every so often we'll stumble into each other, and resume our friendship as though we haven't missed a day. These relationships are important to me on an emotional level: given that you cannot pursue every friend every day, it is great to know that the friendship is still real and available when needed.

As you may notice in this book, some of my best friends have started as business partners and grown to be much more. I think it's a fine idea to make friends of your business partners, but I do caution people about being too quick to make business partners of their friends. Just because you enjoy someone's personal company doesn't mean he or she would be skilled at managing a business. As soon as you hit a speed bump, if your friend doesn't have the same business mindset or skills or abilities as you, the resulting tension could well undo the friendship.

4. Education

In 2010, I was both delighted and surprised to receive an honourary doctor of laws from Royal Roads University. I was surprised because my early university career was less than outstanding. After earning scholarships in the first years, I barely graduated from the college of engineering after failing Reinforced Concrete, not once but twice. I was delighted with this honourary degree because the ideals of Royal Roads—the promotion of lifelong learning, dynamic entrepreneurship and inspired leadership—are ideals that I share and have committed much of my life to achieving. Royal Roads has a motto that I admire and have adopted into my own life: "Living our Learning." This phrase gets at the powerful impact ongoing education has on our work, and the ripple effect that can result. Lives are transformed, business sectors revolutionized and whole communities are made better by the power of ongoing education.

And that's why one of my own personal values is to never stop learning. I have a plaque on my desk with a quote from the artist Michelangelo who, at the age of eighty-seven, said, "I am still learning." This man, who was considered by many to be at the pinnacle of artistic achievement during his lifetime, never got to the point where he thought he could stop learning. I try to model that same attitude in my life and encourage others to do the same.

One of the reasons I've become involved in the sports, entertainment and various real-estate industries—not to mention the dozens of new business ventures I have invested in through Dragons' Den— is simply because I love learning. Being exposed to interesting people with new ideas who challenge me to embark on another steep learning curve is fun for me. And the more unfamiliar the content, the more fun it often is.

Time spent learning is never wasted. I may use very little (and maybe none at all, as some engineers might observe) of my technical engineering training on a day-to-day basis, but I always use my ability to read, learn, and absorb and analyze new ideas and information on deals or businesses or charities that are presented to me.

I had an early love of finance, and during my time in engineering school, I studied the *Financial Post* newspaper from cover to cover. It was a great education about the real world of business. Eventually, some friends and I started an investment club. There were nine of us and we each put in $200. At the time minimum wage was $1.65 an hour, so $200 was a fair bit of change for us. We just pretended we knew what the stock market was all about. We spent some time figuring out how the market worked and the simple things about it: buying and selling, paying a commission, starting to follow research, starting to understand market trends. At the end of the day, each of us got back $221 for our $200 investment, so we felt that we had been successful financially, but more importantly we were successful in terms of process. Those were the early days. But it was a start. And as my learning about finance grew, so did my skill. The real point I am making is that there are learning moments or opportunities around you at all time—you only need to be ready for them.

I truly believe that the three most important subjects everyone should study are marketing (because everyone needs to know how to sell themselves and their ideas), entrepreneurship (which is really about innovatively meeting needs) and philanthropy (which is about social investing). I believe that if every student left formal education with these core subjects, it would have a tremendous impact on both the business world and on our communities generally. I discuss this key-courses concept in greater detail in a later chapter.

Education doesn't stop when you leave a formal study program. That's why I'm willing to look at mistakes as lessons rather than failures. Life experience is one of the greatest teachers, especially for young people. Travelling the world, volunteering in the community, facing challenging situations and being part of a competitive sports team are just a few of the opportunities available to us for lessons that will shape the mind and character for the better.

Learning is the best way to achieve life and business goals because, when you stop getting better, you also stop being good.

5. Career

As part of my reassessment of what matters in life, my career now comes towards the bottom of my list of priorities. I still work hard, but I work even harder at breaking my work addiction by maintaining a schedule that allows more time for myself, travel with my children and downtime at my cabin and other destinations with friends and partners.

During my parents' generation, career paths were pretty straight. It wasn't unusual for someone to spend his or her whole working life at the same job. My own circuitous journey is a reflection of the new work/life reality. It troubles me how fast we push students to choose a career path. The author of the *Lord of the Rings* trilogy, J.R.R. Tolkien, wisely wrote, "Not all those that wander, are lost." I often speak to high school and university students, and I tell them not to worry if they don't yet have a clear plan to pursue a narrow or specific career. It's okay to study liberal arts for a year or two. Spend time studying subjects such as the history of world politics or religion. Or take the opportunity to travel. The business world can wait for your arrival. I am fond of sharing my belief that there is lots of time before the need for overtime.

It takes time to figure out what you can uniquely offer to the world. As mentioned, one of my daughters studied engineering, worked in the Caribbean for several years and is now on her way to culinary school. It's better to slow down and wait for the passion to develop than to jump into something that isn't the right fit. Chasing a parent's dream isn't the template for a fulfilling life. And remember, wandering doesn't mean you are lost.

> *"Spend time studying various subjects like the history of world politics, or religion. Travel. The business world can wait for your arrival. It takes time to figure out what you can uniquely offer to the world."—WBW*

For some, a job is a way to pay the bills and feel proud of doing an honest day's work. For others, what they do in the day is a path to personal fulfillment. Your career doesn't just have to fill your bank account. It can also fill your spirit. Whatever you choose, do it with passion and do it full-out—and the rewards will become obvious in time. I love the challenge of doing deals. My love for innovation and marketing gets fulfilled in the multitude of relationship-building events that FirstEnergy hosted annually and the trademark events (i.e., the Garden Party) that I now do on my own. I get energy out of my enthusiasm for planning new approaches to life.

No matter what the career, I believe everyone should develop an entrepreneurial mindset. As a society, we tend to think that entrepreneurs are people who graduate from business school. But anyone can have an entrepreneurial mindset and innovation can happen anywhere.

Whether you're an employee or an employer, an artist or an account-ant, you can find ways to innovate and be part of the creative process.

Innovative thinkers are constantly asking the question: how can we make things better? Don't be afraid to think out of the box. Just because something works, doesn't mean it can't be better. No matter what you do, or where you do it, strive to be a pioneer in your industry.

The best career advice I can give is to encourage you to answer this question: how can I use my knowledge, my network and my per-sonal passion to creatively meet the world's greatest needs? No matter what your skill set, I promise you that your willingness to innovate will literally change the world.

6. Community

Once you've taken care of you, your family, your friends, your educa-tion and your career interests, I believe you then have an opportunity to give back to the world at large in whatever way you choose, be it through time, money or the combining of time, money and creativity.

Rather than attempting to guide succeeding generations from the grave, which many people choose to do, why not plan to make a difference right now? Many people with wealth still like the idea of establishing an endowment to provide a legacy after death. To me, that idea is wasteful. After all, once you're back to dust, you're dust. It's arguably a strategy to memorialize one's life, fed a bit by ego, that I don't think optimizes one's contribution to the world. I would encourage more donors to work with their lawyers and wealth advis-ors to find a more efficient way to use their charitable dollars—and to find a better balance between giving today and giving tomorrow—rather than waiting for death to resolve the issue. I also believe the charitable sector would greatly benefit from a change in tax regula-tions that would require foundations to disburse more of their assets annually. Currently, foundations are required to allot a minimum of 3.5 percent of their total assets each year; this is maybe a third of what I would like to see forced out in distributions! Changing the world takes cash today and tomorrow. Quality projects always find funding—eventually—so don't over worry the day *after* tomorrow.

On the other end of the spectrum, those just starting out in their careers, or those with young families, often delay donating cash until they feel they can afford it. But as Mother Teresa said, "No act of charity is too small." There are roles for everyone in charity—and government plays a key role.

> *"One of the best ways I know to find real and lasting significance in life is to enrich the lives of others."—WBW*

In thinking about giving, consider the government-driven tax incentives. Tax considerations aren't the primary motivator for many donors, but, as reported by Statistics Canada, the proportion of Canadian tax filers claiming charitable donations is declining. Imagine Canada, a national organization representing charities, has indicated that more than half of Canadian donors would increase their giving if there were better tax incentives.

Never before have there been so many positive ways to help create the kind of communities we all want to live in. I hope at least one of these initiatives helps get your money out of your wallet—or from under your mattress—so that you can experience the true joy of giving while living.

Balance Passion with Priorities

I've learned that a successful life functions well on both a business and personal level. Just as successful companies have business plans, successful individuals should have personal plans.

The six priorities I listed above represent my personal business plan. Some people are surprised, given all my charitable efforts, that community is the last of my six major priorities. For me, focusing on health, family, friends, education and career have to come first. Nothing matters more than my health and personal relationships. A commitment to constant learning and pursuing my passion in business come before charity because they provide the leadership and resources from which I am able to give. I am an active philanthropist but I truly do put community last on my list of priorities. The other aspects of my life *must* be considered and taken care of before I can truly give to my world. I do make time for all.

I work at maintaining these priorities constantly, and I have a number of close friends and colleagues who challenge me to think through my decisions based on my stated priorities. One of my closest friends, Kimberley Amirault, is a sports psychologist who is often the voice of reason and logic in my life. She is a long-time friend who has been instrumental in helping me in my own pursuit of happiness. Also instrumental in my journey is Hap Davis, a psychologist who has worked with me from time to time since my run-in with cancer in the early 2000s. A key part of my support team. Another friend, Kathryn Dundas, who was originally "just" my doctor, has transcended that role through the connectedness of the health journey outlined above. She has become one of my closest friends and confidantes on every level. Believe me, she knows how to keep me accountable! And then there is my personal coach, Keith Hanna, whose approach to organizing my thinking about business, personal and family relationships has been pivotal in many successes. Lastly—but not really last—is Joni Avram, who is my personal coach in respect to philanthropy, brand development and management and speaking messages. She is an invaluable and appreciated resource for me almost 24/7.

The difference that setting priorities has made in my life can't be measured. It's helped me greatly improve my relationships with my children and share deeper, healthier relationships with the people I care about most. It's helped me be healthier in every aspect of my life in my fifties than I was in my forties. And it's helped me continue to pursue my love of business with passionate intensity, but this time with balance.

In many ways, cancer was the best thing that could have happened to me because it truly forced me to slow down and think about how I was living. **Cancer may have saved my life.** Cancer allowed me to say no to every request for my time. I wouldn't need to change what has happened in my life. But I do take every opportunity to encourage people around me not to wait for a crisis to figure out what really matters.

I would recommend that each of you considers the questions I shared earlier that were posed to me not so long ago. First: What would you *like* people to say at your funeral? And then look at what might be the toughest question: What *would* your children say at your funeral?

If the answers don't line up with your dreams, maybe it's time to examine your definition of success—and the priorities you associate with that definition.

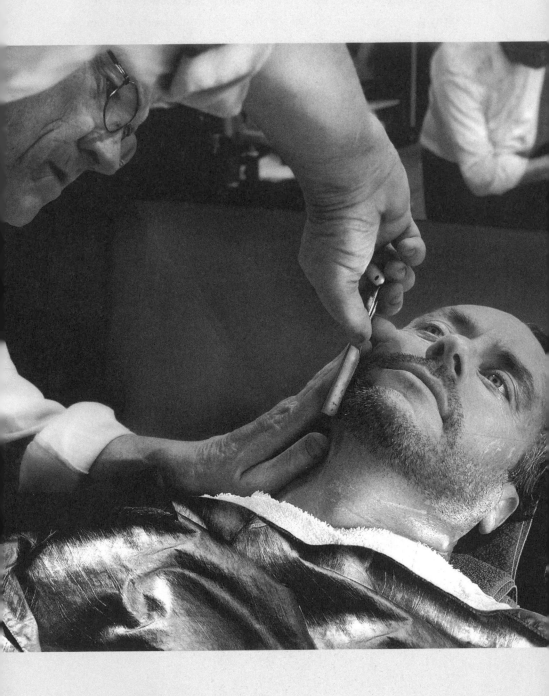

Here is a man naked to the blade.

It's about trust, that subtle agreement. Trust the barber, have confidence in his reliability.

Although Sweeney Todd lurks behind the arras, with his lever and his dangerous chair. Or Buddy Bolden in a trance, a not-barber jazz musician who played his cornet right to death. Or Figaro, the man who sings and dances, making way for the city's factotum, serving up connection.

But here is a moment of respite. Nothing demon or unwitting, just a ritual shave, tilt back and let the footrest do its work, boots and legs reposed, relaxed from their walking job.

Reminders of the old days. Even now, barbers won't let a woman into the chair room when they shave a customer. Too dangerous, all those razors, a wild or angry person can just grab a blade and slice revenge, a few quick cuts and all discussion ended.

Throat vulnerable, open. The exact position of the edge, touching the skin but flirting with air, passing just that millimetre from blood. Badger hair and bristle-load all calculate the precise angle of the cut, razor-master at work. While the ears wait out their avoidance and the nose tangs with the smell, sandalwood or lime, no-name or Gillette, the fine calibrations of this intimate service.

The barber—that old guy in glasses, accompaniment, shadow self—has to be trusted.

Exposed face and mouth, supine legs, require that bravest of all desires, pure trust.

Only true confidence shakes hands with trust.

—Aritha van Herk

Four

Choose Integrity

During the Depression of the 1930s, in the middle of the great bald prairies, when dirt was flying off the fields and 30 percent of the population couldn't find a job, a small school was born and began to thrive in Wilcox, Saskatchewan, a small town just south of Regina. Under the direction of Father Athol Murray, affectionately known simply as "Père," and aptly described as "a salty character with the mind of a scholar, the vocabulary of a dockworker and the soul of a saint," the school emphasized the values of good character, leadership and community living. With this solid foundation, Père was able to take a bunch of kids, who some said were headed for nothing but trouble, and turn them into highly regarded scholars and world-class athletes. Père's great vision, energy and determination helped Notre Dame College eventually gain an international reputation for producing some of North America's greatest student athletes. He taught them that hardship could lead to triumph. The school's motto, "Struggle and Emerge," is still reinforced today.

A few years ago, I was asked to give the keynote address to the Notre Dame graduating class. Addressing the graduates of this storied prairie school was a singular highlight among the many wonderful life experiences I have enjoyed. I toured the school grounds before giving my speech, and was struck by the fact that Père's legacy so clearly lives on in the hearts and minds of the people he continues to touch, so many years after his passing back in December 1975. That legacy, and its impact on future generations, is what happens when you invest your time and energy in support of lasting principles.

Prairie Ethics

A tough country grows tough, resilient and independent people. The Père Murray story is a beautiful illustration of the rock-solid character of this sort of people. Prairie people seem to be capable of overcoming all manner of adversity. There is something about growing up in a land that is as harsh as it is beautiful that has helped create some of the finest people in the world—people who are resourceful, respected and solid to the core. Ask anyone in the Calgary corporate community and they'll tell you: if you want to hire a trustworthy person who understands that a hard day's work earns a fair wage, just hire someone from Saskatchewan. (There is a humorous anecdote often shared in downtown Calgary: What do you call someone from Saskatchewan? The response: usually you just call them Boss. It's a tribute to the business success of so many Saskatchewan imports to the Alberta oil patch.)

Like many people from Saskatchewan, I have a soft spot for home. I'm an unapologetic prairie boy. I have tremendous respect for my prairie heritage and the innovative people who created something out of nothing. What occurred in Saskatchewan in the late 1800s and early 1900s is a great example of Canada's entrepreneurial spirit. In a relatively short time, determined settlers with enormous vision and stubborn perseverance helped turn the wild prairie into one of the most prosperous agricultural economies in the world. Never forget, you can take the boy out of the prairie, but you can never take the prairie out of the boy.

The pride Saskatchewan people share in our province isn't only expressed during football games. It's also expressed in our affection for the land, our enduring optimism that next year will be better than the last, our dedication to community and our commitment to some enduring values that I believe come from prairie roots. My ex-wife, Pamela, was fond of reminding our Alberta-based friends—and I agreed—that the mountains are nice, but they really get in the way of the view!

Cowboy Ethics

I would like to acknowledge James Owen, who wrote the book *Cowboy Ethics: What Wall Street Can Learn from the Code of the West*, for his influence on my current thinking about this fascinating subject. A leading Wall Street financier, Owen became troubled about the growing number of corporate scandals and wrote *Cowboy Ethics* to inspire a return to simple, timeless values found in the West— fundamental principles like honesty, loyalty, courage, respect, commitment and integrity.

In the most basic terms, living by a set of principles boils down to knowing and respecting the difference between right and wrong and choosing to do what's right. As Owen suggests, "There's right and there is wrong, and nothing in between." I know that more than a few business leaders would disagree. They think there's a delicate balance between telling the truth, and telling just enough of the truth to attract investors. They believe that being fair or equitable in a business deal makes you a sucker with a bleeding heart. Or that being a person of integrity is a nice idea, but not always very practical in the business world—following the old nice-guys-never-finish-first paradigm. I simply don't and won't buy that.

I encourage you to take some time at www.cowboyethics.org to get a clearer sense of what Owen is asking the world to embrace as front-line ethics in life and business.

When it comes to integrity, it's a matter of deciding up front what you're prepared to do, and not do. If you want your behaviour to be a source of inspiration for your kids, to continue to earn and deserve the respect of friends, colleagues, competitors and clients, and go to sleep at night knowing that you've done right by the people around you, then it pays to make a commitment to living a life of integrity, based on lasting principles. Because, ultimately, you will not be known by your abilities; I believe you will be known by the choices you make.

The work of Owen is so important to me that I am lifting it verbatim here to share with you to reflect upon. The ten principles below are his timeless cowboy values, all of which resonate with me as a prairie boy to my very core:

1. Live each day with courage.
2. Take pride in your work.
3. Always finish what you start.
4. Do what has to be done.
5. Be tough, but fair.
6. When you make a promise, keep it.
7. Ride for the brand.
8. Talk less and say more.
9. Remember that some things aren't for sale.
10. Know where to draw the line.

Take a Stand

FirstEnergy was inadvertently (as in, we unconsciously or unknowingly accepted them) built on cowboy ethics. We valued the high road and without planning to do so, aligned ourselves with Owen's values. Our reputation for possessing character and integrity and our commitment to excellence helped us outrun the competition as much as, or maybe more than, any other factor.

There is a difference between doing the right thing, and not doing the wrong thing. Sometimes doing the right thing is about more than just following someone else's rules.

When an investment dealer raises money for a company by selling shares to new investors, the dealer gets paid a commission, typically anywhere from 4 to 6 percent of the total raised for mainstream issuers. On top of the sales commission, usually with lesser quality or smaller issuers, some investment banks will negotiate what are called "broker warrants," which allow investment dealers to enjoy extra compensation for lifting the value of a given stock. The inclusion of broker warrants is often considered a lower-end approach to financing for companies that can't otherwise access capital. I often felt that such warrants were extracted unfairly from the company and its shareholders. Broker warrants are controversial to some investors because clients of investment banks look to the dealer for an objective analysis about the quality of any given stock. It can be pretty hard to be perceived as providing an objective analysis when part of your compensation model is based on raising one stock's value.

At FirstEnergy, we always enjoyed a reputation for the quality and objectivity of our industry and company analysis. To avoid any appearance of conflict of interest, and to develop and maintain a solid reputation in the industry, we decided when we founded the firm not to participate in charging broker warrants. We wanted fair wages for a hard day's work: nothing more and—nothing less.

Our decision not to engage in notionally overcharging our clients and remaining objective was simple enough. But our initial decision soon hit a serious snag. We started participating in deals with broker warrants already built into the original contract on deals led by other investment banks. We had no choice but to accept the warrants under the terms of the contract we had assumed. But how could we maintain our commitment to integrity and still honour the terms of the deal?

To solve this conundrum, we got creative. We established the FirstEnergy Community Foundation. All broker warrants—and any income earned on them—were directed into this charitable foundation. Over time, we even began charging early-stage energy companies our own version of broker warrants: we renamed them "charity warrants," and fed them straight into our foundation, in turn generating millions of dollars for the foundation, which we distributed back into the communities where we do business.

We didn't stop there. After we introduced the concept of charity warrants to the deals we were leading, other brokers would seek a share. I still remember advising a participating dealer that the charity warrants were going 100 percent to the foundation to ultimately distribute to charity. His response was, "We are our own charity," and he argued for a piece of the charity warrants for his firm's bottom line. Our response? "No. Not a chance. Never. Forget it. Don't ask again." He got the answer clearly and quickly. And didn't ask again.

> "A person who is nice to you, but rude to the waiter, is not a nice person."—Dave Barry

I'm proud to say that as partners we took the time to debate the merits of broker warrants and looked for a business solution that met with our values in so many different ways. We could have shrugged our shoulders and pocketed the windfall. But channelling the money into charity allowed us to distance ourselves from this sometimes questionable practice, encourage a higher standard from other industry players, and ultimately do something good for our community.

What I learned through the broker warrants challenge was that even if you can't fix or change something entirely to your satisfaction, you can still make it better. You can speak up, raise awareness, set boundaries and say no to what's going on. Your courage and integrity might just inspire the next person to follow your example—or to do it even better.

Doing the Right Thing

In the ordinary course of business at FirstEnergy we often engaged in signing agreements for what were known as "bought deal" financings. Under these agreements, we as the underwriter were obligated to first buy and then re-sell a certain number of shares at an agreed price for our client. Any shares not sold to investors would be retained by FirstEnergy or the syndicate of underwriters led by our firm. Holding such shares was not a desired outcome—ever—but we were simply middlemen facilitating a financing with our own balance sheet to give the issuing client certainty on pricing and timing for funding their business.

Partway through the process on one particular deal, we realized we had misjudged the market and would likely end up losing a lot of money. We were in danger of stumbling badly in attempting to place the shares with credible and supportive long-term investors. Errors made by the client during the negotiations gave us a legal justification for backing out. It was a tempting option. One of our competitors had walked away from a mispriced deal just a few weeks before, much to their reputational detriment, and so we were doubly sensitive about taking the next step.

Walking away from the deal—as we were legally entitled to do—would have left our client with a huge challenge: the market would not be there for a replacement financing for a long time. Staying in the deal would have left FirstEnergy, and the individual partners, with a huge financial loss. News that we had unwound the deal—if we did— regardless of the circumstances, would have landed on every boardroom table in the oil patch.

Rather than backing out, we did what we thought was fair and right. We went back to the client and put our concerns on the table. We argued that since the pricing wasn't accurate, the issue wouldn't be well placed, and the deal wouldn't be in the company's best interest. But we also did something unusual. We agreed to honour our commitment—despite those very serious issues—no matter what. We laid out several options for the client, including voluntarily unwinding the deal, re-pricing it or moving forward as originally agreed. After presenting all the options, we let the client choose. In the end, they agreed to simply re-price the deal so we could properly place it with investors, and everyone walked away happy.

If we hadn't been willing to stand by the spirit and intent of our agreement, I don't believe the client would have given us the flexibility to re-price the issue. Our decision to be fair allowed, and maybe caused, our client to be fair in return. We maintained a positive relationship with that client and, better yet, they told the story to everyone who would listen. As predicted, the oil patch business community heard about how FirstEnergy made a tough decision to do the right thing. The goodwill generated was multiples of anything we might have dreamt possible.

Deal on a Handshake

One of the things I'm most proud of is my willingness to do a deal on a handshake. I always want to be known as a person who can be trusted to keep his word. And I want to deal with the same kind of people. It's amazing how fast a deal can close when the people involved trust each other. The typical cover-your-back chess moves usually employed in closing an investment just are not there when you're dealing with honourable people. When I strike a deal on Dragons' Den, or anywhere else for that matter, my team's working instructions are to do the homework needed (always), but also to look first for ways to get a deal done, and only second or last to be looking for ways to change or drop a deal. I often see people use almost any excuse to wiggle out of a deal, or to renegotiate more favourable terms.

In his book, *The Speed of Trust*, Stephen Covey tells a story about Warren Buffett, considered by many to be a man of the highest integrity. Buffett acquired a $23-billion-dollar company, McLane Company, Ltd., from Walmart. In the normal course of events, a $23-billion-dollar acquisition would include teams of lawyers, accountants and other advisors poring over documents for months and months. But not with Warren Buffett involved. I loved reading that the parties met for two hours, shook hands and the deal was effectively completed. The paperwork that followed was simple, and quickly followed the handshake. That's what happens when honest people do business with other honest people, people who both value the spirit and intent of a handshake.

I'm not saying that I never paper a deal. Not at all. I work to get a deal done on a handshake and move to paperwork in due course. You've got to start somewhere. But my word and my handshake are my bond and more powerful and relevant than any legal contract. Barring any new information in a deal of any kind, after a handshake or a promise to deal, everyone should be committed to moving forward as promised.

FirstEnergy was started with a handshake months before any paperwork was ever signed. The four founders began meeting quietly in the fall of 1992. Over the next few months, our discussions and vision for the company became more and more advanced, and we realized we were onto something. By early 1993, six months into planning the new investment bank, it became clear to us that we should do something just a bit more tangible to confirm each party's interest in forming the partnership. We

> *"I'm most proud of my ability to do a deal on a handshake. And I want to deal with the same kind of people."—WBW*

then agreed to put our money where our mouths were and put up what was at the time meaningful good-faith working capital to fund ongoing expenses: $25,000 each. If one of us wanted out, but the other three were still gung-ho, the full $100,000 would stay tied up in the deal. Anyone who pulled out would lose his upfront investment. All done on a handshake. And that deal turned out to be one of the best investments— and, of course, partnerships—of my life.

I recently concluded a multi-million-dollar investment in the United States. Due to complexity in structuring for cross-border tax issues and various regulatory approvals, the deal took more than a year to move to final closing. As we were re-papering the deal for the umpteenth time, a lawyer for a party new to the process asked for a copy of the signed Letter of Intent—and was stunned to discover that both sides were still at the table, resolving issues as they arose, on the basis of the handshake that was done to seal the deal in the first place.

I would rather do business with people who value the principles of fairness and equity through a handshake than deal with anyone who needs to grind out value from the other side, fighting over minor points throughout the closing negotiations.

Be Fair

Almost twenty years ago I was working on a potential merger agreement between two small companies. I introduced my client to another company that I knew would be interested in merging: the fit was right with assets and management. The only issue was relative valuations. After several discussions, the two companies decided not to go ahead with the merger. They shook hands and parted ways. However, a few months later, they reversed their decision to part ways and proceeded with the merger, but left me, as the advisor who initiated the deal, completely out of the transaction. They suggested that they didn't think I was owed any compensation for the initial advisory work, since that deal had not proceeded. Because I get paid to broker and create merger or acquisition relationships, I strongly disagreed.

When I confronted the original client after the merger was announced, he was defensive. A few months later—in a downtown coffee shop—he offered a tepid apology, saying it really wasn't up to him, but that, "if I had known it was going to be that important to you, I would have pushed to have paid you." That told me everything I needed to know about that person. A few years later, when he came to me with a new business deal, it was pretty easy to move along— no thanks. He underestimated the value to me of a relationship with honourable people.

Your Word Is Your Bond

There's a story in James Owen's book about a cowboy who was about to die. On his deathbed, he made his best friend swear to eventually take his body back to Texas and bury him there. The friend agreed, and the next spring he started the long brutal trip back home, taking more than a year to get there. "Next time I make a promise," the friend related at the graveside, "I'm going to be a little more careful." Because I place such a high value on the promises I make, I am careful not to promise something too quickly.

I take this approach with all my deals. Once I shake hands, I move forward in good faith, fully intending to finish what we started. Once I've agreed, I'll always look for ways to move ahead, rather than scramble for reasons to back out. It's inevitable that there are going to be bumps along the way, but I've noticed that some people will use almost any excuse to withdraw from a legitimate deal.

When people back out of deals, or try to change them at the eleventh hour just for their advantage, it makes me wonder whether that person went into the negotiation in good faith. I just don't think it's fair to wait until a week before closing to ask the deal-breaking question. I'm always amazed when people think they can make a buck by breaking their word; eventually, your lack of integrity catches up and you'll end up paying for it. The nasty or unfair things people do to others start to add up over time. The flip side is also true: when you act with integrity, you'll attract great people and great opportunities.

Be Respectful

One of the key elements of integrity is respect. In addition to following through on my commitments, I also focus on respecting the dignity of others. For me, respect is the ability to value another person, and their perspective. It involves treating people with courtesy and kindness. Respect is not the same as agreement. In fact, it is a basic sign of respect to trust people enough to tell them when you disagree. But respect should dictate how you express your opinion.

I am wary of people who get pleasure from attacking or insulting others. When someone treats others with a lack of respect, to me it says very little about the person they attack, but volumes about their own integrity and insecurity. When I need to give constructive or corrective feedback to another person, I try to avoid personal attacks. On

Dragons' Den, some of my colleagues felt the urge to deliver the *truth* with a certain malicious zeal. It certainly creates "good" television. It seems to be a game for some of them to see how creatively they can challenge or question a presenter. People who like to be brutally honest seem to enjoy the brutality more than the honesty. If you're having fun hurting someone with the truth, I would suggest you back off, think of their feelings, and try to let them keep their dignity.

When I was being considered for Dragons' Den, the CBC producers told me straight out after my first screen test that they were concerned that I wasn't mean enough. I told them if being mean meant being unkind and disrespectful, then I wasn't interested in being part of the show. But if they were looking for someone who could be tough when it actually mattered or was relevant (i.e., not just for television theatrics), then I was the right guy for the job.

Respect is an essential part of a successful company. It's the responsibility of a business leader to foster an environment of respect in the workplace so that line managers in turn treat their employees with courtesy and appreciation. I find that when employees move on, it is often because they don't feel respected.

I am proud of the culture of mutual respect that we cultivated at FirstEnergy and that I now maintain even more at Prairie Merchant Corporation. Of course, the best way to create a culture of respect is to demonstrate it. While I am far from perfect in execution, I do think I know what is right. I try to show respect by following through on my commitments. By listening to concerns, soliciting ideas for improvement and using the good ones. By showing that I value my employees' contribution and time. I demonstrate respect by being polite, honest and willing to engage in difficult conversations. By communicating with confidence but without dominating meetings, I try to show respect by making a genuine effort to connect with people and by understanding what they value.

The ways that I demonstrate respect are the very same ways that I earn respect. I believe in *earning* respect, not *demanding* it. Respect is not a function of title; it is a result of character. Be someone whom you would respect—you will find that you are respected by others.

Learn from Challenges

In the summer of 1999, on the day before FirstRodeo, FirstEnergy's annual fundraising event, a company we had contracted to erect tents on the rodeo grounds showed up late. The tents were the standard variety used for large outdoor events. During set-up, which was done at dusk rather than, as expected, in the afternoon, a metal pole came in contact with an overhead wire and two employees of the rental company were electrocuted, one of them fatally. It was a tragic accident for the people involved and their families. Both the tent contractor and FirstEnergy were charged by the health standards board and subsequently sued by one of the families.

Certainly no one intended this sort of outcome from any client event, and above all, one that was being run to raise money for charities in our community. Although the charges against us were withdrawn and the courts placed all the blame on the contractor, we felt enormous moral guilt over the accident. As a result—and some observers suggested it was an overreaction—we initiated the process of hiring an independent safety consultant for every event we did, indoors or outdoors, so there would be someone to make sure all our suppliers complied with the highest safety standards. Although we couldn't change the outcome of this tragedy, we felt we owed it to our community and to all those we contracted with to ensure safety was an even higher priority than some others thought necessary.

Never Give Up

One of the brightest and best investment fund managers I knew—he was based in Houston, Texas—was a personal friend of mine, one who had supported me through some very tough times. He took his own life rather suddenly during the market meltdown in fall 2008. Stocks were plummeting. He saw his managed funds devalue significantly with material drops in value every day for a month or more. There was no logic to the new market valuations. Sadly, he couldn't see past the downturn to remember that every valley has two sides. I wish I had known the depths of despair he was facing at that time and been able to reach out.

A lot of Albertans, especially those in the oil industry, are familiar with roller-coaster economies. From the late 1970s to the early 1980s, Canada's energy policy was designed to keep domestic oil prices artificially low—at levels well below the world price. The plan was a benefit to oil-consuming provinces but a big blow to oil-producing provinces like Alberta. Oil royalties were redistributed, which meant a smaller share for producing provinces. Government incentive programs rewarded Canadian firms for finding oil on federally controlled rather than provincial lands, lowering provincial production. These policies became a lightning rod for western anger, but there were underlying issues at play, including inflated housing and commodity prices, that finally led to a severe economic downturn in the mid-1980s. There were layoffs everywhere. Stock prices fell. Housing prices slumped. People walked away from their mortgages. Does any of this sound familiar? Anyone living in the West at that time will vividly remember the challenging economy they experienced.

"Never be afraid to fail. Be afraid of not learning from mistakes."—WBW

The tough, optimistic and resilient nature of Albertans meant that the majority of people stayed the course and found their way out of the economic valley. Companies restructured, new companies formed to take advantage of new opportunities and individuals and families found ways to live on less. Not only did we recover from economic calamity, we eventually created one of the most prosperous economic booms in history. And such cycles seem to just keep coming to the West.

Everyone faces hardship, disappointment and failure from time to time. But to succeed, you have to make a commitment to never give up. Like Père Athol Murray's students at Notre Dame, you might find that your greatest hardships lead to your greatest triumphs. And maybe most important of all, don't hesitate or be afraid to share your issues or concerns with those close to you. I have always loved the line from Dr. Seuss: "Those who matter don't mind, those that mind don't matter." The reality is that your true friends (including those that are family) will always be there for you. Find them.

Here is a man deciding how to play.

The guitar's neck is like a woman's, the supersternal notch waiting for touch. That hollow dent where the clavicles converge, or the collarbone gives way to softness. What does that mean? Directory precision. Do not digress.

The frets on the guitar require tender attention, knee and hands cradling incipient notes behind the door of memory.

How to strum sound from wood and stone? Is there a perfection of touch, a tension that resounds tone?

Notes fall in ambient riff, pitched to the colour of the day, the duration of instrument and key, the closed door, the patched heart.

This is a man of definite modulation, that intricately recognizable air sprint that collects memory in its brief refrain. Cluster and sequence, then repeat, the notes retracing a path known but forgotten.

Ostinato: stubborn repeat. And repeat. The figure expecting improvised variation and returning to origins, that comfort of recognition. Memorable, a quality that will not let the phrase escape, but brings the notes back in their particular configuration and leaves them shimmering in the air, recalling the tingle of first hearing.

—Aritha van Herk

Five

Go With Heart

I've noticed that the people who make a lasting contribution to the world always seem to find and follow their passions. If you're not passionate about the business you're going into, you're likely never going to succeed. Anything you do out of a sense of obligation is going to have a different outcome than when you act out of a sense of opportunity. It all comes back to passion. Which for me lies within my heart—and guides my decisions!

Move Your Limits

In my late teens, I encountered an experiential learning program called Outward Bound, a four-week-long wilderness adventure that required me to endure gruelling physical challenges, fatigue, hunger (including a three-day solo journey) that pushed my physical, mental and emotional boundaries to new limits. Surviving a month in the mountains gave me a new sense of confidence in my abilities. The obstacles and hardships I faced helped me deal with many of my own personal fears and insecurity. Until completion of my own Outward Bound experience in 1977, I had never really felt comfortable in my own skin.

The Outward Bound challenge forced me to deal with the unknown, to meet challenges and learn about teamwork. Most of all, it taught me about my own potential. As a philanthropist, I have supported Outward Bound for years because I believe so strongly in the life-changing process of experiential learning—especially in the outdoors—that can help young people identify their respective gifts, discover higher levels of self-awareness and self-confidence and develop a greater desire to achieve more in life.

Bolstered by my own sense of confidence, I went on to pursue my two personal passions: entrepreneurship and philanthropy. But there was one other source of inspiration in my entrepreneurial journey— my great-grandfather.

Explore Your Roots

The development that occurred in Saskatchewan and across the great Canadian prairies in the late 1800s and early 1900s is a great example of entrepreneurial spirit of the West. In a relatively short time, determined settlers with enormous vision and stubborn perseverance helped turn the wild open prairies into one of the most prosperous agricultural economies in the world. The people who pioneered the prairies—from the hunters and trappers to the farmers and the fishermen—were truly our great nation's early entrepreneurs.

One of those early entrepreneurs was my great-grandfather, J. Benjamin (Ben) Prince. He was my father's grandfather. Prince was born in St.-Grégoire, Quebec, and came west in the late 1800s. He eventually settled in Battleford, Saskatchewan (across the river from what would be my birthplace and childhood home, North Battleford), and built the first sawmill there, and later, the first flour mill. The original diversified investor, he also opened a department store and was an active farmer and innovative rancher. In fact, he was one of the first ranchers in the West to breed and raise cattle expressly for shipping to European markets in the early 1900s.

Prince was also a highly regarded political leader. He represented the Battleford region in the legislative assembly of the Northwest

Territories (whose boundaries were re-drawn when the provinces of Alberta and Saskatchewan were carved out). He went on to become the mayor of Battleford, and was eventually appointed in 1909 by then prime minister Sir Wilfrid Laurier to the Senate, where he served until his death in 1920.

Understanding the history of Saskatchewan, and my family's role in developing the province, was a great source of encouragement for me as a young and aspiring entrepreneur. When I realized that one of my forefathers accomplished something remarkable, I knew it was in my blood to pursue the same dream. I have a strong psychological attachment to my great-grandfather and have sought to follow his lead in my own small way as a builder of our great country.

> *"Canadian pioneers—the hunters, the trappers, the farmers and the fishermen—were the original entrepreneurs. Celebrate them!"—WBW*

Set Expectations

One of my first entrepreneurial experiences was cutting the lawn of the elderly widow next door when I was entering my teenage years. My dad suggested I take on the job, and since I had a friend who was making $2 per cut, I knew it would be a good way to earn great money.

My mistake was in not negotiating or confirming a price up front. Instead, I went ahead and started cutting her lawn twice a week, about thirty cuts in total over the summer. When I went to collect at the end of the season, she invited me in for a cold pop, proudly handed me $10, and asked what I would spend it on!

I was speechless. I was holding $10 instead of the $60 I was expecting. But that experience was priceless in terms of what it taught me about communicating and establishing mutual expectations up front. In hindsight, it was a valuable learning experience that helped me establish some strong negotiating fundamentals and expectations later on in life.

Identify the Opportunity

As a student at the University of Saskatchewan, I became quite active in student politics. One of the roles I secured was vice president, social, within Voyageur Place, the on-campus student residences. To accommodate the larger events we hosted on occasion, we had to go off-campus. Since the downtown venues weren't within walking distance for most of the students, we knew we had to solve the transportation issue if we wanted to make the downtown events more attractive to attend.

Together with my good friend and roommate, Daryl Rudichuk, who was also president of the resident association, we came up with a perfect solution: we would rent city buses. They could pick the students up at the residences on campus and deliver them back home at the end of the night, eliminating concerns about finding a cab, or drinking and driving. Enthusiastic about our idea, we presented it to the rest of our student council. We got at best a chilly response. The executive came up with a list of reasons why our plan wouldn't work. They thought we stood a good chance of losing money, losing students, or both. They simply didn't want any part of it because of their perception of the risks involved.

Daryl and I believed the plan would make us money, and so we took a risk on our first entrepreneurial adventure together. We saw the risks as very manageable. We rented two buses at something like $35 each for the night (remember: this was 1978) and charged each student $1 round-trip. Since a one-way cab ride was almost $4, we immediately attracted dozens and dozens of customers. The bus shuttle was so successful that we ran our little business a number of times over the course of the year on "downtown party" night. When most of our friends were earning around $2 an hour in a minimum-wage job, we were doing well enough financially that we could afford to take cabs to and from the downtown dances rather than ride on our own buses!

Following Passion

One of the best choices I ever made was the decision to go back to school to pursue an MBA in entrepreneurship. I had been working for just over three years as a petroleum engineer for Imperial Oil. I knew I was a good engineer, but I didn't feel I would ever be a great engineer. I just wasn't that excited about continuing in that role. While my interest in running engineering projects was fading, my interest in running the whole show was growing.

As part of my grand plan, I let my bosses know that I wanted to join the ranks of management. In response, they did what many big bureaucracies do to enthusiastic employees—they sent me for a test. It was called something like the "Leadership Aptitude Test," and it was designed to measure my leadership or management abilities as measured by a large corporation such as Imperial Oil. I failed spectacularly. At least, in my mind I failed. I was told in no uncertain terms that I was not management material. The test confirmed that I was a strong technical engineer, which was great news for Imperial because they needed people in that role. Following the test, the company wanted to continue to slot me into engineering positions. That suited them but it really didn't suit me, or my growing passion for business. I declined.

> *"If you are not passionate about the business you're going into, you are never going to succeed."—WBW*

Ironically, my apparent failure in that test was the best thing that could have happened. It was the kick I needed to go back to school and pursue what I really loved. Until that moment, further education was on my nice-to-do list. It wasn't that urgent. After getting my test results, getting an MBA instantly moved to my must-do-now list.

What I didn't realize at the time was that the test measured my leadership abilities within a large bureaucracy. I learned over time that I *did* indeed have meaningful leadership qualities, but they could only be expressed in the right environment—an entrepreneurial environment, such as a small, nimble start-up. Being able to absorb information, make decisions, and watch the whole ship turn according to my direction was what really excited me. It turned out that being in a large, sometimes slow-moving and very bureaucratic organization (like most large companies) wasn't the right fit for my temperament or talents.

I can't say I fully understood what I was getting into when I went off to do my business degree, but I knew that my personal inclination was leading me to doing an MBA in entrepreneurship at the University of Calgary, and to a new, interesting and very rewarding world.

Making Waves

The day we launched FirstEnergy in the fall of 1993, we ran a series of print ads with a headline that was meant to be as fun as it was provocative. It said: "We are not here to test the waters. We are here to make waves." Created by Rich Thompson, who is now a close friend, and his creative team at Zero Gravity Inc., this advertisement was designed to let Canada's energy industry and the related finance sector know that we intended to do business in a new and aggressive way.

Before FirstEnergy came along, oil and gas companies needed sizeable assets, usually well over $100 million dollars in equity value, before any of the bank-owned investment dealers would deal with them. A few regional or boutique firms were working with small cap companies (i.e., anyone below the $100-million level), but the large investment banks systematically refused to touch them. They didn't even try to hide their arrogance as they turned down business from hundreds of these smaller companies, telling them that they needed to grow in order to be worthy of the bank dealers' attention.

FirstEnergy was designed to take advantage of this incredible untapped market. Unlike the big banks, we would be organized and staffed to provide investment banking services to *any* oil and gas company, no matter its size. Our timing was perfect. We were at the front end of the wave of small players eager to take advantage of property rationalization opportunities in the lucrative energy industry. We were now establishing relationships with a number of growing smaller companies who were run by really strong management teams. Our early interest in their early-stage success was ultimately a key element of our own long-term success.

See What No One Else Sees

As with all entrepreneurial endeavours, the bigger the problem you solve, the bigger the reward. One of the big problems facing the oil and gas industry was the complexity of owning oil and gas properties and the associated inefficiencies. The challenge originated in a now archaic concept of risk-sharing between energy companies. With any one section of hydrocarbon-prospective land owned by a dozen or more companies, and with any one discovery potentially covering ten or twenty or more sections of land, the resulting oil and gas discovery could have more than one hundred different owners. The complicated ownership then greatly increased overhead and administration, and dragged out approvals for further capital investments in the property. All in all, it was an extraordinarily inefficient way to run an industry.

It didn't take long for the small companies with access to equity capital to start to purchase the overhead-burdened oil- and gas-producing assets that were beginning to be consolidated in the early 1990s. For the most part the majors—the largest oil and gas companies—started to rationalize their asset portfolios by selling off their fractured interests in properties they couldn't control effectively. The nimble juniors started buying smaller property interests and consolidating them, until ultimately they held 100 percent of a given property. They then began to enjoy the incredible efficiencies created by simplifying administration and streamlining decision-making, including the all-important capital optimization opportunities (i.e., reinvestment decisions). Another upside came from what I call "fresh eyes": the review of previously virtually ignored properties by new owners who had a very clear financial interest in finding and unlocking hidden value.

The opportunity created by this consolidation led us to pro-actively seek out new management teams, often coming out of the majors, to run the newly formed and financed oil and gas companies. As these new start-ups became more efficient and began to accumu-late greater assets, they would either sell off to larger companies or merge with someone of equal size. With each move, FirstEnergy would help in various ways, from structuring the new company to coaching the management on corporate governance issues, includ-ing strategic selection of members for the new board of directors. Then as each company evolved, we helped them find new sources of financing and access to capital they hadn't previously been able to lay their hands on.

Under the old model, a boutique investment bank like FirstEnergy might work with a small cap producer until the company outgrew the investment bank's balance sheet and research capabilities. Eventually, once the company had grown, a larger, bank-owned dealer would inherit the client relationship. FirstEnergy's approach was to grow with the client so we could maintain the relationship from original inception to final sale.

This approach allowed us to build intimate and strategic rela-tionships with hundreds of small cap firms that the big banks had turned away. We were happy to do the smaller $1- or $2-million early stage financings and create clients for life. FirstEnergy became the first investment dealer to provide an integrated research, investment banking, sales and trading platform for small-to-large capitalization energy companies.

Over the course of our first fifteen years in business, FirstEnergy has participated in literally thousands of financings and M&A pro-jects totalling well over $250 billion. Rather impressive when you consider that this was all from a small group of passionate and dedi-cated professionals—all in their mid-thirties—toiling in downtown Calgary. And all because we were the first firm to go after a huge market no one else saw or wanted.

Questioning the Status Quo

As you might expect, launching FirstEnergy led us down an often obstacle-strewn path. Navigating the registration process with the Toronto Stock Exchange (TSE), the Alberta Stock Exchange (ASE) and the Investment Dealers Association (now more properly known as the Investment Industry Regulatory Organization of Canada), which were at the time the key bodies that regulated trading in debt and equity in Canadian markets, was among our earliest and more interesting challenges. We knew the application process could be a long, unpleasant grind, usually taking up to six months. Because we wanted to avoid such a long delay and—above all—to avoid or delay disclosing the identity of key (and new) partners, Murray Edwards turned to me and asked a key question: "I get that they say the approval process can take six months, but why does it take so long and what can we do together to make it more efficient?"

We were told that submissions were always reviewed in great detail and were always found deficient in a variety of ways, some small, others large, but all had to be sent back to the applicant for supplemental information or revision. Once the application was updated, it would have to be reviewed again and then returned yet again, even if there were only minor flaws. We were told it was just the nature of the process.

We stepped back and saw a potential solution: we asked if we could submit our application in draft form (i.e., unofficially), and have the ASE identify any deficiencies up front. That would delay the public disclosure of our key initial partners (Davidson and Grafton) and accelerate the actual approval process once the almost-final application had been submitted. Based on their feedback, we submitted our application in draft, and asked them to review it for us. The ASE agreed to do so, knowing that we were 100 percent serious about creating a significant investment bank. By the time we were ready to apply formally, we really had a flawless application. By thinking a little differently, we shortened the then six-month process in which you had to expose your business plan, including the names of all key partners, to all of our competitors, down to a few short weeks.

Embracing Risk

I enjoy a drive to innovate. I love to do things that haven't been done before. To do things in ways different from the ways others have done them. No new product or service would exist if someone didn't have the courage to try something new. But innovation involves taking risks.

The key lesson or aha! experience I got from my entrepreneurship studies was that entrepreneurs are not risk-takers per se (as I mentioned in respect of the decision to start on my own), but rather that they view risk differently. Entrepreneurs have to be confident and tenacious but they also need to do their homework. I think every great entrepreneur thrives on *calculated* risk. Entrepreneurs simply perceive risk differently.

> *"Entrepreneurs are innovative thinkers who are constantly asking the question, How can we make things better?"—WBW*

Risk isn't something to be feared, it's something to be managed. In the early days of my first business, Wilson Mackie & Co., Inc., there were times when Jamie and I had to break piggy banks to make payroll. A second mortgage on my home and an operating line of credit got me out of a few tight pinches in terms of covering operating overhead.

Taking Calculated Risks

Early on in the life of FirstEnergy, a client with whom I had developed a close personal relationship offered us the opportunity to finance their purchase of 10 percent of an oil company operating in South America. I saw it as a very risky investment because they didn't control the asset, and warned the client against moving ahead. I argued that because he couldn't control the property, and didn't know who the partners really were, there were too many variables to make the investment opportunity attractive, regardless of the upside. He thought about it, and decided that the property had too much potential to let pass. Rather than buy only 10 percent, and based in part on my belief that we could finance assets such as the one he described, he decided to mitigate the risks of minority ownership by buying the whole property!

He called me late one Friday to see if we could back the new deal that had finally come together that morning. He needed a deposit of $5 million by the following Tuesday, and so we had to figure out how to finance the deal over the weekend. The client and I spoke a number of times and then met on Sunday to talk through options. He drew out the whole deal on a large cloth napkin (which I still have). He drew the country, the maps, the oil properties and he explained the exploration upside. Trusting his innate intelligence, and having confidence in my own instincts, I committed personally to invest $1.25 million (which was pretty much the extent of my available wealth at the time), which in turn convinced one of my wealthier partners to commit another $1.25 million. We were halfway there.

Then I went to the rest of my partners and said something like this: We know that no retail client or institutional investor will ever touch this deal based on the facts. The assets are in South America, and the buyers have never operated in South America. In fact, they've never actually drilled any oil wells outside of Canada. The father-and-son team doesn't yet have a CFO. Or a management team. On top of the money they've already put into the project, they now need a $5-million deposit by Tuesday. There is no research published by anyone on the company and it has a market capitalization of less than $20 million. We'll lose the deal and the relationship if we can't raise the rest. It's a bet on the father and son. An unconventional bet, for sure. Any interest?

Over the next few hours, my partners committed personally for another $1.5 million bringing us to $4 million in hand. Together, we made some calls, and eventually found four institutional or "private wealthy" orders totalling the final $1 million. The additional financing was leveraged entirely on the strength of our team's personal orders, which in turn came on my faith in the entrepreneurs we were backing. By the time Monday afternoon came around, we had raised the $5 million. The issuer knew that in the normal course of affairs, this funding would have been almost impossible to arrange, and that we had just made a huge leap of faith in backing them.

Over the next five years, that initial investment grew in value by more than twenty times. As partners, we took a huge risk on a father-and-son team and a foreign project that no one else would touch. A lot of people (including my partners) questioned the logic of the investment, but for me it was a calculated risk. I trusted the client and believed they could pull it off. I knew that no one else would invest the money they needed. The South America deal was the biggest and most lucrative deal of my career to that point in time.

As FirstEnergy, we effectively became the founding financiers of this company when we helped to raise $5 million when their company was valued at $20 million. And we were the key M&A advisor less than five years later when we sold the company for almost $1.1 billion (yes, that was *billion*). Obviously a lucrative relationship for all involved.

Mixing Business with Pleasure

Work and play don't always have to be separate. When I invested in some 20 percent of the Derby County Football Club, an English Championship–level football (a.k.a. soccer) club, a lot of people close to me had just one question: Why, Brett? The question was often repeated a year or two later when it became known that I had invested—initially at the 5 percent level, and subsequently horse-trading my way up to 12 percent—in the Nashville Predators' National Hockey League franchise in Tennessee.

After meeting with the respective management and ownership groups, I couldn't help but admire their commitment and vision.

And after I did my homework, I realized that there was an incredible amount of passion and history behind each team. Both enjoy an extraordinarily loyal fan base. My decision to invest in professional sports was looking at a business decision that could be wrapped in fun. I don't want to sit around the fireplace on Sunday night and review my stock certificates. I would rather be in the game—regardless of the game. No matter what business you're in or what investments you make, life is too short not to have fun with it all. I don't get overly emotional about any of my investments. I am always willing to invest incremental funds alongside my partners if additional funds are required, or, if the opportunity is compelling, to liquidate some or all of the investment.

Here's a man we all want to meet, down at the local laundromat.

Laundromat blues, all steel and burnished instruments, efficiency compliant. The laundry pretends to do more than it can, erase desire, melt the dirt of the day, the night's alluvium. Here is where we unload the burden of apparel, the clothes that tame us, wear our habits of eating and sleeping, restless movement. The round drums symbol their circle, infinity's unbroken line, while linens toss restlessly within, approximating white, some definition of clean.

The consoles number mechanical miracles, positioned for work, temperatures hot and cold, directives on soil. These machines are sturdy squares of wizardry, promising flight, the erasure of effluent, skin and its tegument becoming a vanished trace. Laundromats offer a way to disappear, a fade path.

There is nothing more intimate than laundry, soiled clothing or clean a connection, a revelation, a touch and a trance, how crisp it all seems coming out from the machines. Ready to take on the world.

And this man, as neatly ironed as his cuffs, as beautiful as a peacock, not-singing the laundromat blues.

—Aritha van Herk

Six

People First

Partnering with the right people is the best way to find lasting success and satisfaction in business and on a personal level. While it seems obvious, it's not that easy to do. Whenever I think about investing my money, I'm normally far more interested in the person than the project. I've learned that it pays to invest in people because smart, honest people will make money almost anywhere. Yes, accidents and mistakes do happen, but good partners drive over speed bumps without turning them into mountains.

No one comes to the table with everything they need for building a successful business. Often the most successful people are the ones who've built a team of partners to help them along.

Being part of a successful team is more valuable to me than having complete autonomy or independence. My passionate belief in the value of teamwork is directly connected to my commitment to lifelong learning and accomplishment. Members of high-performing teams grow to new levels by learning from each other. Partners don't have to share the same title or position on the organization chart. Partners are rarely equal in all skills or interests. But they do have to share the same vision and commitment to a shared dream to be effective together.

The best partnerships I've had always have a mix of experience and talent. In the average partnership, one plus one equals two. But in the best partnerships, one plus one can truly equal eleven. Whatever you do, choose your partners wisely. Bad partners are not just liabilities, they are anchors. When you're struggling in your partnership, energy that should be invested in the business gets expended on wasteful friction. In reality, there is always a beginning and an end to every partnership—and ideally they are not that close together!

"The best way to find out if you can trust somebody is to trust them."—Ernest Hemingway

At the core, every good partnership has to be built on trust. Because I place a premium on being trustworthy, I am quick to assume that others do as well. I tend to see people as trustworthy until they prove me wrong. If someone betrays my trust, it's a very hard thing—in fact, almost impossible—to restore. And I have a long memory. Sometimes I can be too quick to trust others, but, with experience, that issue has become less of a challenge. Besides, I would rather be seen to be trusting than skeptical of everyone's integrity.

Nevertheless, the kind of deep trust I've built with most of my business partners didn't happen overnight. While it's possible to trust someone up front, more often it builds with time. It builds with mistakes and shared experiences that can survive the inevitable challenges life presents.

Tallest in Character

I met John McCann through my small group forum in YPO. He was a mentor to me through many of the personal challenges I faced in the late 1990s. He was a rock of support, so when the opportunity came to invest in his company, The Bolt Supply House Ltd., we quickly struck a deal. Without already knowing John well at a personal level, I likely would not have invested in his company. What I invested in was John and his knowledge of his business, and, most importantly, in his ethics, values, leadership style and skills.

John has a unique approach to doing business. Even though he sells fasteners and industrial supplies, he will tell you he's really in the people business. He has a great deal of emotional intelligence and uses fun rather than fear to motivate his staff. There is a tremendous focus on family at Bolt Supply. If their kids are in a school play, employees are encouraged to take most of the day off—not just to watch the play—but also to be with that child as part of their support team before the event. Employee satisfaction is high and staff turnover is modest, a sign of John's extremely effective leadership. By focusing on people, he's built an army of totally engaged employees who keep attaining higher levels of effectiveness. Bolt Supply has one of the best ratings in our industry sector in North America for profitability per employee. Low staff turnover translates into an equally strong client retention rate and annual sales growth.

Since my initial investment more than a decade ago, the top line of the firm has more than doubled and the bottom line has gone up by a factor of ten. The value of my original investment has grown by four or five times. Today, my annual return on investment is roughly equal to my initial investment. That's the value of investing in people over projects.

Here's what John had to say about our relationship:

Brett is a very dynamic soul, and I say *soul* because he puts his heart and soul into everything he does. I would describe his partnership style as "Mr. Straight Arrow." Always do what you know is right and success will follow. He places a high value on recruiting the best people and treating them with dignity and respect. As he says, he "bets on jockeys and not racehorses," and "a company is only as good as the people it keeps and the customers they attract."

Brett is a handshake guy, his word is golden, and he is a cut-to-the-chase individual who gets it quicker than anyone I know. His genius crosses a wide range of interests. Brett has taught me to squeeze a lot more into life. His schedule is always full speed ahead and by surrounding himself with winners, he can pass the ball and know it will be well handled. In troubled times, he is empathetic and understanding; he is compassionate and fair. He is the real deal—for me, a dream partner and friend.

People Are Essential to Your Business Plan

Just as John does at Bolt Supply, at FirstEnergy we also tried to develop a family-type environment. Unlike most other investment banks, we worked to promote work/life balance throughout the company. The quality of life and general well-being of our employees is important to us. We have also avoided an overly hierarchical structure, encouraging employees at every level to share their ideas freely with everyone else.

On the career page of FirstEnergy's website, you will read our claim that, "Our focus is energy, but our passion is people." This statement isn't just recruitment rhetoric: it's the foundation of the company. One of the biggest assets you will ever have, and the one that appreciates the most, is the human capital you hire, develop and retain. I admire any firm that recognizes that its core assets ride the elevators.

In my experience, people are always willing to stay later, work harder, apply themselves more creatively and invest their hearts in the cause when they know you're also investing in them. Below are some general ways that I use to identify and work with good partners—people with character and integrity who make doing business not only profitable, but fun.

Look for Passion

I want to do business with people who are passionate in every aspect of their lives. For most successful people, hard work and enthusiasm are usually evident in everything they do. I don't buy that people have different morals and values in their personal lives than in their business lives.

One of my key business heroes or mentors is Richard Branson. I admire his creativity and his passion for his brand. He grew up battling dyslexia, and he wasn't a great student. While he was only a teenager, he stepped into the world of the entrepreneur. Ironically, his first successful business was a magazine called *Student*.

Today, he's the founder of Virgin, one of the most recognizable brands on the planet. From the early days of his music business to launching an airline and being an innovative philanthropist, Richard Branson keeps setting his sights on new challenges and then mastering them. I see his point of differentiation in all of his businesses as his genius-level grasp of every aspect of marketing. He is the kind of person I aspire to be, and the kind of person I would like to do business with. I have enjoyed the privilege of his company several times, at meetings on his private island, to discuss his views on changing the world. Let's just say that his retreat—Necker Island in the British Virgin Islands—is a great place to listen.

> *"I invest in people, not projects. I watch for passion, integrity and insight—smart, honest people will make money just about anywhere."—WBW*

Closer to home, a man of passion whom I greatly admire and respect is a veteran of the Calgary oil patch, Clay Riddell. Clay is one of the icons of the energy industry, having built one of the most successful independent oil giants, Paramount Resources Ltd. (He was the founding-level investor in many successful oil and gas companies.) Now in his seventies, he still works full-time, is hands-on with several major companies, and is actively engaged with passion in all aspects of his life, from community-leading philanthropy to working closely in various business ventures with all of his children, and he still finds time to attend his grandchildren's social events. He has clearly figured out how to do it all. With style and character, Clay is truly a role model demonstrating how to pursue dreams with passion.

I like doing business with people who have practical experience rather than book smarts. When I'm hiring, I'm rarely impressed by someone who has nothing more on their resumé than academic credentials. I'm looking for extra achievement, whether it is participation in a choir, Boy Scouts, travel, volunteering, sports or politics. I don't care what your choices are, I care that you've made choices and haven't just been watching life from the sidelines.

Know What You Know (and What You Don't Know)

I am leery about working with people who have quick, easy answers for everything. I especially watch out for people who pretend to know it all—or even worse—*believe* they know it all. In my mind, instant answer might equal instant fool. Rather than pretend to know something they don't, the people who impress me are the ones who say, "Let me check on that and get back to you." It is a simple statement that only enhances credibility. It's easy to see when people are making up an answer on the spot. If they had only admitted that they hadn't yet done enough research in a particular area, or hadn't thought of the issue, they might actually walk away with investors who are competent business partners, and who could help them expand their market. I have a lot of respect for people who admit when they don't know an answer. But I don't want to hear that answer twice on the same issue when it is relevant to their business!

Too many eager entrepreneurs exaggerate the value or potential of their business as they attempt to gain investors. Even worse, their lack of insight into their product's marketability comes off as either unforgivable ignorance or willful deception. A few simple questions will usually leave them fumbling for answers as they trip over their numbers and try to cover their lack of knowledge. It's a bad equation. Even if a product or service has great promise, no one wants to do business with someone who is ambiguous or uncertain coming out of the gate.

"Watch out for people who pretend to know it all. If you don't know, say so. It's a simple statement that only enhances credibility."—WBW

One of the things I liked about being on Dragons' Den was that it showcased the breadth of talented entrepreneurs across the country. There are many bright, innovative business people in Canada who just need a bit of help with resources and guidance to get their ideas off the ground. Unfortunately, there is also no shortage of people with poor fundamentals who are looking to attract investors by embellishing the facts. If you want to get ahead, do your homework, and be honest about what you know and what you don't know.

Look for Demonstrated Integrity

The best partners have a history of demonstrated integrity. Anyone can put on a mask and fake it for a while, but spend enough time with him and he'll reveal his true colours. Character is often revealed in the smallest actions, not only in the big ones.

One individual with an exceptional history of demonstrated integrity is David Richardson, my second-in-command and president at Prairie Merchant Corporation, my private merchant bank. He is a man of his word and his personal reputation for integrity is such that I've never had to second-guess him. I trust him so completely that he has enjoyed single-signing authority on behalf of Prairie Merchant since shortly after he started with me—and long before I asked him to be the president of my operations. He's been with me, with the goal of protecting my back, through every significant deal I've done in the last decade.

Think Mutual Interests

I'm interested in working with people who are fair and honest, people who will do the right thing even if it means taking it on the chin every now and then, and people who keep their respective interests at heart. They aren't looking to see how they can profit at someone else's expense.

John Brussa is the kind of person who works with mutual interests in mind. He is a brilliant tax lawyer who has structured virtually all of my more successful business deals. He also, incidentally, invented income trusts about two decades ago.

Around the time we started Wilson Mackie, we needed a place to set up shop for a few months while our offices were under construction. John invited us to move in with him at his law firm, which was located directly across the street from my new office space, making it a perfect location to work from while we did our leasehold improvements.

We were eager to accept the invitation. It didn't matter to me that the space he was talking about was actually a tiny boardroom. Some of John's partners weren't amused when we started entertaining potential clients out of their offices, but John had faith in me and asked his partners to cut us some slack. The offer of space for "a month or two" was extended several times while our office renovations dragged on.

This not-so-small gesture by John had an enormous impact on me. Over time I more than repaid his faith in me by sending his firm referrals, legal work and branding for his firm, as well as co-investment opportunities that resulted in millions in revenues for both sides.

John is an amazing business partner and friend. His impact on my personal life is as significant as his impact on my business life. We have never papered a single deal we've done together until the final closing. It is a testament to the high level of mutual trust, a quality that John shares with his entire client base. Because we are always focused on mutual interests, when the time comes to discuss compensation, we have actually argued in favour of the *other* person. Rather than trying to squeeze every dollar out of each other, we focus on being fair and treating each other the way we would like to be treated. Respect for the other guy's interests and a focus on the long term is the foundation of our relationship. And we've both succeeded as a result. It's a great way to do business. I quite enjoy the mutual admiration and the fact that we *never* get to saying, "I owe you one." Friends just don't have to keep track.

Here's what John says about our relationship (with a bit of legalese):

In business, as in relationships, opposites sometimes attract. Most observers would agree that Brett and I have diametrically opposing styles. Brett has boundless energy for whatever he is tackling and takes an action-oriented approach to problems. I am more reserved and likely more cautious. Notwithstanding the differences in style, I would like to think that Brett and I share many core ethical values in how to deal with opportunities and problems. Hence, notwithstanding the outward contrasts, we have had many a fruitful business partnership and a close personal relationship over more than twenty years.

In many ways, I think the partnerships we have had reflect Brett's approach to life. Brett is incredibly open to new experiences and to people who do not necessarily share his style or background. He also recognizes that life is a team sport and that you cannot have a championship team with only one type of player. No Stanley Cup champion has had twenty-three stay-at-home defencemen or twenty-three flashy forwards. It is the mix that makes you successful, shoring up your weaknesses with the strength of others. I have learned to be a better businessman by taking that approach to heart.

I will give you just one example of his inclusiveness. Likely Brett's greatest achievement was the launch of FirstEnergy, along with several partners, in the early 1990s. I had a small hand in the launch and that role evolved from a chance meeting with Brett at a time when he was, at best, a casual acquaintance. Brett was telling me about a venture that he was considering and I told him that my law firm had just moved into new premises and if he wanted to slum with a bunch of lawyers for a while, we could probably find a place for him to hang his hat while he pondered his next move. That was ultimately the start of Wilson Mackie, which was later rolled into FirstEnergy and, as they say, the rest is history.

Through Brett, I was welcomed as a member of the FirstEnergy family from the outset, a relationship that endures to this day.

That chance encounter affected my practice immeasurably in that I was automatically included in, and had access to, Brett's incredible Rolodex of Calgary business. Brett showed me many kindnesses in introducing me to a broad cross-section of his contacts and that was one of the pillars on which my practice has been built. All of this for a person who did not, at least outwardly, share Brett's approach to business. Brett continues to this day to be a loyal friend.

Play to Your Strengths

When Murray, Jim, Rick and I got together in 1990 to talk about starting FirstEnergy, we didn't just plan what we would do. We also planned *who* would do *what*. As I explained earlier, we built the firm based on the strengths of each of the four partners. The planning process took place over some nine months, with team meetings every two weeks and countless weekend meetings and cellphone calls.

Because we had spent so much time together, we came to understand each other well. We knew one another's strengths, and we played to those strengths, letting people focus on what they were especially good at.

Play Up Your Personalities

Another element of our business plan where we excelled was to build the firm's profile in unconventional ways. We were a bunch of thirty-something mavericks with more than a little attitude. And we played up that attitude. We gained a reputation for being smart and aggressive. In Calgary style, we had a reputation for throwing some of the best parties in the city, all in support of local charitable initiatives.

We sought to do common things in an uncommon way, and that garnered us considerable attention, which in turn helped to grow the firm. In the process of building the firm's profile, we also got behind and celebrated the individual successes of each of the partners along the way, which was another critical component in our collective success.

Expect Conflict

The best partners have skills that cover your weaknesses. Pick people who complete the team, rather than compete with the team. It's inevitable that you will share some skills. But when skill sets overlap, disagreements also are bound to occur. When a group of strong-willed high-performers gets together, expect to bump heads every now and then. I've always encouraged respectful disagreement and debate. Differences of opinion usually lead to better results.

The partners of FirstEnergy have worked hard over the years, but we've also fought hard. We've celebrated together, criticized each other and coaxed one another along. More than anything, we have always been passionately committed to the firm and to its mission. And that has helped the firm succeed as much as anything else.

Plan Transition/Succession

FirstEnergy's focus on the right partners has helped us make the successful transition from an entrepreneurial start-up to a well-managed company—another substantial accomplishment. By putting people first, FirstEnergy has attracted the kind of talent that can grab the baton when it is passed, setting the firm up for successful transitions from one management group to the next.

A testament to the success of that focus is that in the first fifteen years of the firm's operations we only had to terminate the relationship with one partner. In that same time, we had only ever hired two people from competitors to join the partners table. The rest were all, as they say, "homegrown," individuals who came up through the ranks internally.

Make Friends of Your Partners

Many of my strongest friendships have developed out of my business relationships. Jeff Kohn is a real-estate developer, and ours is an important friendship that grew out of a business partnership. Jeff really understands the value of a handshake. We've done many millions of dollars' worth of real-estate deals together. Because of our mutual trust, almost 100 percent of the work that is done before closing a co-investment deal is done on the strength of clasped hands.

While many of my business partners have become personal friends, very few of my friends have become business partners. One notable exception is Murray Edwards. Murray and I connected through student politics at the University of Saskatchewan. At the weekly meetings of the students union, we'd contend over topical issues of the day, ranging from photocopier salesmen (a big issue on campuses in the late 1970s) to fending off the then apparently growing presence of the student-based Communist Party. Our friendship continued even when we began our careers in separate cities. He has become one of Canada's most successful entrepreneurs, and I am privileged to call him a partner in a number of ventures and a long-time friend/advisor.

Spouses as Partners

I have come to appreciate the great multitude of partners in my life, and there have been many to be grateful for. The first and most important partner in my life has been my ex-wife, Pamela. Together, we set up the groundwork for three absolutely amazing children. As I indicated earlier, her influence in grounding them, in helping instill in them strong morals and values, continues to make her an indispensable partner as a co-parent.

Pam was my first true love. We met at university during my third year of engineering school—her second year—and, yes, I did take advantage of the fact that I was marking papers in one of her classes to arrange to meet her. We were married a few years after graduation and settled in Calgary to pursue our careers and raise a family.

During our marriage, we both went back to university to do MBAs at the University of Calgary. She graduated higher in her class than I did, evidence of her considerable acumen and academic proficiency.

Quite quickly we discovered that Pam was highly skilled at recruiting and interviewing. In the early days of Wilson Mackie, she organized all the hiring. She would conduct interviews as Pam Janzen (her birth name). Eventually the recruits would realize that the boss's wife had just hired them. New employees were often surprised and fascinated by our working relationship.

I trusted her in this role because Pam understood me, she understood our business and she understood our vision. She was skilled at taking a hundred resumés, culling to the top ten, and eventually handing over the top three prospects. On more than one occasion, instead of hiring one, we would hire two of the top three. We were only looking for one, but she consistently found great people.

As enduring proof of her talent in this area, there are still people that I am partnered with today who came out of those original interviews. And most of those she recruited or shortlisted have gone on to lucrative careers in the energy industry.

As a wife and business partner, Pam did an extraordinary job. While she was an engineer with an MBA, giftedly smart, who could have pursued her own career goals and ambitions, she chose instead to play a pivotal role in building our companies. And our family. The success of the businesses certainly benefitted the entire family financially. Because her work revolved around certain key aspects of the businesses, she had more flexibility and time to focus on our three children, which was invaluable to our family.

Seek Mentoring in All the Right Places

Early in my career, I was privileged to work with many people who invested their time in me, more than a few of whom have become icons in the Canadian finance industry. I learned many lessons from these masters, and my appreciation of their talent has only deepened with time.

One of the first people to play a major mentoring role in my life was Jim MacDonald. Jim was the managing partner in Calgary for McLeod Young Weir. Jim was well connected in the Canadian financial community and commanded a tremendous level of respect internally. He was responsible for hiring me into the world of investment banking.

He was a voracious reader who knew what was going on in every major business sector in Canada. He had a reputation for finding unusual solutions to the various problems that might arise during a merger-and-acquisition deal. Jim's reputation as a brilliant dealmaker attracted a large number of clients to the firm. Jim taught me to open my eyes and see creative opportunities that were invisible to others.

Another man who has been influential in my career development is Dan Sullivan. I worked closely with Dan on several real-estate projects during my time in Toronto with McLeod Young Weir. Dan took the time to demystify the world of investment banking for me. Despite being considered a guru of Canadian real-estate finance, he amazed me with his willingness to teach, and he showed tremendous patience throughout the training process. Despite his senior role, he took the time to explain the meaning of every clause in a document, and taught me simple but important skills such as how to manually blackline documents so that edits could be properly tracked. Many prominent real-estate players in Canada wouldn't make a move without consulting Dan. Given the level at which he operated, I was fortunate to work with him so early in my career.

And I learned grace under pressure by working with David Wilson (no relation). David was one of the architects of the sale of McLeod Young Weir to the Bank of Nova Scotia and went on to play a senior role at what became known as ScotiaBank, before assuming the significant position of chairman of the Ontario Securities Commission.

David managed the transition from an independent investment bank to operating as a division of a huge commercial bank. On a good day, guiding the firm through that process must have seemed like herding cats and kangaroos. But he was able to keep everyone moving in one direction, manage egos and never lose his cool. He was a master communicator, adept at keeping everyone informed at every step. His confidence and calmness only enhanced the power of his communication. He just never got rattled. Whenever I face situations that threaten my good humour, I think of David's grace and diplomacy under pressure. By watching David, I learned that when you lose control, you lose. David set a great example for many to follow.

Pay It Forward

The lessons I learned from mentors have stuck with me and made me a much better person overall. Having so many talented people take the time to mentor me has inspired me to mentor others, including my own employees. I know that when a senior person invests in a new recruit, that attention makes a big impact, building confidence and loyalty to the firm. It's also exciting to watch people grow over time and eventually join the ranks of the partnership.

I've also enjoyed mentoring people whose businesses I've invested in or partnered with. Here are a few stories about the value of mentoring in the words of several of my partners.

Mark Watson, Earth Innovations Inc.:

> Since becoming a shareholder and director of Earth Innovations, Brett has become a mentor and inspiration to the EcoTraction team. His ability to give us his focused, undivided attention while juggling the pressing demands of his other business interests, family commitments, philanthropic endeavours (and now celebrity life) continuously astonishes me.
>
> In our first encounter, what distinguished Brett as a possible partner from the other Dragons were two things. The first was his unique ability to quickly put his finger on the pulse of our business. While others shamelessly bargain-hunted for opportunities to "squeeze our heads," Brett took a far more holistic

approach in his line of inquiry. He clearly wanted to know us and our business, rather than show off his knowledge or humiliate us.

The second lesson I learned from Brett was that when fundamental agreements are forged, they must be respected, regardless of whether additional personal advantage can be gained. When some of the other Dragons tried to change the terms of our agreement after five months of intense due diligence, Brett firmly held his ground and said, "This is not how I do business. My word is my bond and I honour my commitments." I firmly believe that much of Brett's business success is founded on the power of his moral integrity and that his timeless principles underpin why he is one of Canada's brightest and most visionary entrepreneurs.

In an era where capitalism is shifting from destructive self-interest to more sustainable and compassionate economic-growth models, Brett personifies a new way forward for entrepreneurship and responsible risk-taking. Brett wears his passion for life, for business, for excellence on his sleeve every day. He reminds us of the importance of hard work, staying fit, eating well, making time for loved ones and being committed to continuous personal growth in all aspects of life.

Rachel Mielke, Hillberg & Berk:

Brett and I have been business partners since September 2008. Although he invested in my designer jewellery company, Hillberg & Berk, through Dragons' Den, our partnership is so much more authentic than I expected from a reality television show. I have always believed that Brett treats me with the same level of respect and expectation as he would his largest investment partner. The confidence that Brett has placed in me has pushed me to excel in business and take my modest jewellery company from $100,000 in sales to well over a million in just three years.

Despite Brett's demanding career he always takes the time to meet with me to discuss the future growth of H&B. The things that resonate with me about dealing with Brett are his "prairie ethics" approach to business, his commitment to community through philanthropic endeavours and his zest for life. Not only is Brett a mentor and business partner but also a constant source of inspiration to me. Brett is proof that ethics and compassion do have a place in business.

Marissa McTasney, Moxie Trades Ltd.:

Moxie Trades Ltd. is a Canadian company that creates and delivers workwear for women. After two years of manufacturing and distribution to three big box stores, I negotiated the largest deal ever done in Dragons' Den history (to date). Originally turning down the deal on TV, Brett Wilson said as I was leaving the set, "Call me and I'll help you!" and so I did.

Brett bought out my previous business partners and gifted me with 1 percent of the company to make us truly 50/50 partners. Within six months of signing papers, two of our biggest clients negotiated for exclusivity. After a few months of deal-making, January 2009 delivered a huge setback to our company and both retailers withdrew product commitment, one even cancelling an order three weeks before delivery.

With monthly operating expenses eating away at the funding commitment from the original deal, I was devastated and thought the end was near. Brett's advice: "Stay the course." For months, I re-strategized, developed a new line of products, and built a team to support the new business that would surely come. We pre-sold to many clients and were able to raise additional funds from Brett. I was also able to construct a deal with our logistics partner who agreed to purchase our inventory. This mitigated risk between all parties involved and gave Moxie an opportunity to get back in business.

The lesson I have learned the most from Brett is that integrity is a choice and brings you along and further in business than anything else. A motto that serves well in life and business: "Those who have nothing to hide, hide nothing." Brett has always made it clear that if you don't know, just say so. I believe it is also a great attribute to know what you don't know. In these cases, ask for help.

My choice is to continue searching for the path to balance. That's one thing I haven't learned yet, but do strive for. In terms of my personal life choices, I wake up happy, I learn every day and I am proud of the journey. My measure of success is in my kids' happy dance so I'm good to go. It will be great when we make lots of money though—I'm looking forward to that too!

Carol Welsman, Jazz Singer/Pianist:

I have always viewed the music business as exactly what it is—there's music, and there's business. I'm also an artist who is entrepreneurial and Brett is my role model. We met when he reached out to me following one of my concerts where I had performed a song that seemed to touch him deeply. That was more than a decade ago and we have been close personal friends ever since.

His extraordinary success is no accident. I approached him with a music project in 2009—a tribute to Peggy Lee CD. As the owner of my own record label and in a time when few record companies are spending money on marketing, my dream was to have enough capital to produce and control its development in the marketplace. While I have been fortunate to have achieved a level of success in Canada, this project would also mark my first real foray into the U.S. market, where I have great ambition.

A serious branding man, Brett understood and recognized the potential to strengthen my brand, encourage CD sales and forge exciting new opportunities. I am happy to report the vision came to fruition. The CD was chosen Top 5 Pick of the Year (of all genres) in *USA Today*, and garnered a Juno Award nomination for Best Jazz Vocal Album, plus numerous other accolades. We're on a roll! Brett's backing also enabled me to shoot a music video of the title track, "I Like Men!" which he even took time out of his incredibly busy schedule to appear in.

This is the link to Brett's first music video appearance— www.WBrettWilson.ca/CarolWelsmanVideo

Brett is a man with no airs, who recognizes and embraces talent, opportunities and potential. I'm truly fortunate he believes in mine. His unwavering support has given me more drive to succeed than ever before. This may very well be the project to give me the exposure in the United States that will allow my career to flourish over the next twenty years. I am forever grateful.

Dan King, President, Zero Gravity Inc.:

As the creative director at an advertising agency, you approach your first project with an investment banker with more than a little trepidation.

They're not known for being dynamic, leading-edge marketers. Brett is the exception to this rule. He was the first client to send me back to the drawing board because an idea wasn't risky enough—and for a Christmas card, of all things. The next round of creativity found us taking a swing at Finance Minister Jim Flaherty and his decision to tax income trusts that landed FirstEnergy on the cover of national newspapers. Typical Brett.

What he taught me through that and similar experiences is that good really is the enemy of great. Because when you work with Brett you learn the importance of crafting even the smallest details—the style of a $5 lanyard is just as important as the $50,000 website.

Brett has also shown me the power of collaboration. He's like a movie director when it comes to pulling on the strengths of those around him. Rarely will you receive an email from Brett addressed solely to you. Typically it's sent to several, copied to even more. He seeks input, opinions and advice, taking the best ideas and respecting all contributions.

Am I a better person for knowing Brett? Without question. The way he shares of himself, not just by making donations, but with his time and energy, his success and failures, forces me to look in the mirror and ask the hard questions: Can I do more for my family? My community? Can I do more to make a difference? Brett often says it's about giving all that you can and then giving a little more. And he's said it often enough that I'm starting to believe it.

Mentor from a Distance

Mentorship doesn't just build better employees or business partners; it also builds better people who become better parents, friends, and community members. By celebrating individual strengths and passing on skills and knowledge, we make our business sectors, and whole communities, stronger.

I do believe that mentorship is vital to business success. But it's possible to be mentored by someone without them even knowing about it. I don't have to be in contact with the likes of Richard Branson to be mentored by him. He mentors thousands of people by his actions. Buy the books of the people you admire, study their actions and walk in their footsteps. Given the incredible volume of material (i.e., print and video interviews) now available on the internet, you don't need a direct physical connection to find and work with the mentor of your choice.

Reap the Rewards

Passion, drive, intelligence, trustworthiness, mutual interests and complementary skill sets are some of the most important qualities I look for in my business partners and demand of myself. These qualities have helped me attract and retain some of the best business partners in the world. Together, we have created tremendous wealth, a succession of well-run businesses, lifelong friendships and many treasured memories. It's the best way I know to find lasting success in business.

Here is a man posing.

Not a poseur but a posture, stance arranged according to occasion, the akimbo arms retro to the max.

Assume the post. Ladies to the right and to the left, vamping their wares.

Who's the mannequin here? The red chairs or the gestural fingers or the rows of trousers performing backdrop, waiting to be worn, crying out a destination and a function.

Shoes laced and quick, shod for swift flight, ready to run, and while you're at it, tune an ear to the coming bump in the night, the surreptitious pose, the gilded arm, dressage and the mount.

Let's imagine an imagination. Let's spring for a wheat field and escape this shiny leather, these plastic smiles, faux eyelashes and torchy jet propulsion. Tamed ears and retroussé rib cage.

Prairie ethics, jeans, and turtleneck, and the replica facade playful, witticism and jest, a wisecrack.

Taking it off. Putting it on. This man is downright funny.

—Aritha van Herk

Seven

Tales from the Den

Through three phenomenally popular television seasons, I thoroughly enjoyed my role as a member of the Dragons' Den panel. This nationally broadcast reality TV show, which originated in Japan and was popularized by the British, won two Gemini awards during my three season tenure on the show. Each season, the show presented a new crop of always hopeful, sometimes hapless, entrepreneurs who were eager to bravely pitch their business ideas to five pernickety investors: the Dragons. Some left the Den with new capital and new partners; others went away with nothing but bruised egos. What are the secrets to success in the Den? Having a good idea, knowing your product and market, and being realistic about what your business is worth should be obvious—but they are points that are often overlooked by nervous pitchers.

While I have been critical of the theatrical rudeness the show sometimes celebrates, Dragons' Den brilliantly promotes entrepreneurship across Canada. And its growing popularity (something over two million viewers each week in my last season—four times the number when I joined in 2008) is evidence of how much Canadians are embracing the entrepreneurial spirit. The show proves that there are many bright, innovative business people in Canada who just need a bit of hopefully constructive feedback and some capital to get their ideas off the ground.

As I travel, I get inundated with questions about Dragons' Den. Among the most common questions are why I decided to say "I'm in" to some projects, and "I'm out" to others. But mostly fans want to know how my various investments are doing now, and what *really* happened after the cameras stopped rolling.

After some fifty-five episodes, sixty-plus deals in the Den, and thirty-one deals signed in the real world, I'm proud of my reputation as the leading dealmaker on the show. Based on what we could find online, I've made twice as many deals as any other Dragon worldwide. So why am I willing to jump in on deals that other Dragons often snub? And why am I able to turn those initial offers into signed deals after the cameras stop rolling?

In reality, my approach to investing has nothing to do with being nice. It has everything to do with paying attention to people. I've learned to invest in people rather than projects, and I've become pretty good at picking winners. I'm looking for people who know their stuff, who are 100 percent trustworthy, and who are willing to work hard. Those are the people who usually are going to make a profit. Sounds like a pretty easy combination, but it can be hard to find. When I think I see it, I usually make the deal. The challenge with investing via Dragons' Den is the extremely limited initial exposure allowed in the studio, making it hard to judge the merits of the entrepreneur in question.

"I take a portfolio approach to investing. I don't expect to win them all. Some investments will fall flat, and others will return many times the initial investment. That's the way it works. Don't fight it."—WBW

Although I've got a pretty good investor sense, I don't expect every deal will make a return. For various reasons, some investments just don't work out. Fortunately, I have the balance sheet to take a portfolio approach to investing. While some will fail, others may return from two to ten times my initial investment. And the really great ones will eventually become iconic brands, both in Canada and elsewhere.

In any deal, it's inevitable that there are going to be speed bumps. Sometimes during the due diligence process, the initial valuation of the project doesn't stand up to scrutiny. In those situations, I'm inclined to keep the initial faith I had in the person, and find ways to keep going, rather than reasons to back out—modifying the deal rather than walking away from it. That's how I've managed to sign with so many great people along the way.

I hope this chapter will give you some insight into the art of the deal, and give you a behind-the-scenes look at the ups and downs of Dragon entrepreneurship. But mostly, I hope it will inspire you to be part of the great entrepreneurial mindset that is rapidly growing in Canada thanks to the seeds of entrepreneurship being planted by one remarkable television show. The deals are gathered here in alphabetical order.

3twenty Solutions

3twenty Solutions builds modular housing structures and storage solutions on worksites for the mining, oil and gas, construction and industrial markets. These structures are built out of shipping containers, making them relatively inexpensive but durable, mobile and even stackable. Their market is large and expanding: twenty thousand beds are needed in Saskatchewan mine sites alone over the next three years. 3twenty came to the Den in the very early start-up phase, with a very short—but still impressive—track record. They came looking for a strategic investor, one who could provide capital, guidance, credibility and connections. They found several Dragons willing to jump on board.

The 3twenty team asked for $115,000 for 25 percent of their company, a valuation based on sales of $70,000 in the first month, and projected at $500,000 for the year. All the Dragons agreed their idea was a winner. After rejecting a competing offer from Kevin, 3twenty took my offer of $120,000 for 25 percent. In due diligence we recognized that 3twenty didn't need all the capital at once, so we restructured the deal: I took 10 percent of the company for $50,000 up front, and we negotiated an option to buy another 10 percent, which I have now exercised. I knew of this company before they came to the Den because they had won the first-ever Idea Challenge sponsored by the Wilson Centre for Entrepreneurial Excellence out of the University of Saskatchewan. Even though these young guys looked like they had just started shaving, I appreciated the novel way they were solving a significant problem for many businesses. Given their energy, passion and vision, I believed they could make it work.

Based in Saskatchewan, 3twenty designs, manufactures and installs modular camps and offices. They operate in a 30,000-square-foot shop where on any given day twenty-plus people are hard at work. The company is on track to double its 2011 revenue. In addition to supplying hundreds of bedrooms and offices to western Canadian mining and oil and gas companies, 3twenty launched a rental division to accommodate a skyrocketing demand for rental inventory. Additionally, in an effort to become the leading camp provider in Saskatchewan's north, 3twenty and Pinehouse Business North have formed a key partnership to service northern camp needs.

"Ask anyone in the Calgary corporate community, and they'll tell you: If you want to hire a hard-working, trustworthy person, hire someone from Saskatchewan."–WBW

One thing they sort of forgot about was the number of staff members who would be away from the shop for camp installations, leaving the managers to fill in by swinging hammers instead of managing projects. They're learning how to work *on* their business instead of *in* their business. They've now hired an office coordinator and shop supervisor to allow them to focus more on design and project management.

One big new development is a joint venture that allows 3twenty to own and operate the camps. Ownership of the camps provides recurring revenue and maximizes profitability for the company. Since much more project management is needed, the partnerships are key to success.

One of the best things 3twenty has done is to focus on creating a proud and empowered workforce. With a team that varies from 50 to 70 percent aboriginal with an average age of twenty-six, they've made it a priority to support diversity—and to create a fun environment. An early goal was to emulate the culture of Google within the manufacturing and construction industry. Workers are involved in all parts of the production process and are recognized as an integral part of the 3twenty story going forward.

Ironically, the biggest disadvantage the 3twenty team has is youth. "Picture a couple of twenty-five-year-olds in a boardroom," they say. "We get a lot of skeptical looks. Our relationship with Brett brings credibility. If they didn't believe in us before, they do once they learn he's on our team." Having only recently given up their day jobs to focus on 3twenty full-time, they have big plans to grow 3twenty into a large multi-million-dollar business with a sizeable presence in Canada, the United States and the world. I have no doubt they will make it happen.

The 7 Virtues Beauty

When Barb Stegemann presented her entrepreneurial journey in the Den, it was one of the few times anyone had moved the Dragons to tears. Through her company, The 7 Virtues Beauty Inc., Barb has developed a brilliant approach to social investing. The company sources organic oils from suppliers in countries at war or in strife, such as Afghanistan and Haiti, pays farmers full market value for the oils, which come from orange blossom and other crops, and then turns them into extraordinarily beautiful perfumes, produced in Canada and sold to North Americans. By harnessing women's buying power to help people in rebuilding nations, the business provides employment to hundreds, proves the value of doing business in those countries, and encourages farmers to produce essential oils from legal crops. Illegal Afghan poppy crops account for 90 percent of the world's heroin, which attacks families and communities everywhere. With a business that's helping to build peace, Barb is showing the world that rebuilding is more exciting than destruction. In a way, The 7 Virtues perfume offers peace in a bottle.

Barb is the first woman from Atlantic Canada to negotiate a deal in the Den. She was fearless, getting a deal on a valuation of $500,000 with only two months and $30,000 in sales behind her. Beyond money, she came in looking for a mentor. Jim, Arlene and I all agreed to help. The very next day, I had her booked to speak at a national Young Presidents' Organization meeting in Winnipeg. Since she wanted more than just money, she told me I was the mentoring match she was looking for.

Due diligence took less than a month. Out of the gate, Barb took the capital investment of $75,000 for 15 percent and ordered a run of 10,000 perfume bottles. With a boosted inventory, she immediately started cold-calling department stores. Within weeks, she landed a relationship with The Bay. The chain test-marketed the product in six stores over Christmas. By March, the perfume was in all ninety-one stores in Canada. Her relationship with The Bay allows Barb to provide a more stable market to farmers, making their relationship with her even more valuable. To date, she's invested $80,000 in oils sourced from farmers

"Character is doing the right thing when nobody's looking."—J.C. Watts

in Jalalabad, Afghanistan, one of that country's poorest communities. The humanity behind Barb's company cannot be understated. She has created a product that supports a cause I am deeply committed to: the people of Afghanistan and our troops who serve there.

But this isn't charity: Barb is buying oils from farmers and turning them into a top-quality product. Made with true organic oils, her fragrances are very different from most North American perfumes—and made without paraben (a chemical preservative) or animal testing. These perfumes provide a lighter, but lasting, scent that doesn't walk into the room ahead of you.

While she could easily sell her perfume for more, her fair-trade approach allows farmers to earn fair market wages while also allowing customers to buy at a fair price. Clearly, Barb's character, integrity and passion are the basis for her success.

Barb has a unique combination of skills: she's a creative visionary who can also execute. In fact, she has so much energy that I need to have a coffee before I see her, and a nap afterward. But she doesn't get ahead of herself. Highly influenced by the ancient book on strategy *The Art of War*, she believes in studying carefully first and executing with strength, an approach I fully endorse. Too many entrepreneurs fail because they try to run before they can walk.

Barb has encountered very few political roadblocks on her journey. She's worked closely with the Canadian International Development Agency (CIDA) and the Peace Dividend Trust, organizations that are already on the ground finding business opportunities in these countries and matching them with business owners such as Barb. She's surprised that there isn't a lineup of entrepreneurs to take advantage of these opportunities and is actively encouraging more people to follow her example.

Barb says, "Brett's investment helped me establish a strong relationship with The Bay, which is very special. Shelley Rozenwald, Chief Beauty Adventurer at The Bay, is a veteran of the industry who believes in our potential to become one of the next global fragrance brands. The three of us have created a beautiful chemistry as partners because we all know and respect our individual roles. In addition to these partnerships, my focus is on maintaining strong relationships with suppliers. We want them to know we really care, and that our mission is to take their exquisite products and showcase them to the world."

Unlike many business people who try to grow too quickly, Barb is doing it right by solidifying the Canadian model before going into the United States, focusing on improving every detail of operations—down to point-of-purchase displays. Of course, her major focus is on the people she ultimately wants to help. Through her company, Barb continues the work of her dear friend, Captain Trevor Greene, a peacekeeper in Afghanistan who was brutally attacked by a Taliban rebel. What started off as a way to support troops and farmers in a war-torn country has expanded to touch the lives of countless others. For Barb, success is more than personal. "A lot of people are depending on us," she says, "and we don't take that lightly."

Cosysoles

Like a lot of entrepreneurs, Allan Kotack found a business by solving a bigger problem. Allan's wife, Patricia, is afflicted with a progressive neuromuscular condition called Charcot–Marie–Tooth disease. Patricia's feet were always cold—and painfully so—which made getting a good night's sleep nearly impossible. Thermal socks and battery-operated slippers just didn't work. Patricia decided she needed a slipper with a heating pad that would stay put over her entire foot. Allan and his daughter sewed a pair of slippers fitted with microwaveable grain. They worked! Patricia was ecstatic. Warm feet meant she could go to sleep at night. "What a blessing," she said.

Allan soon realized that millions of people around the world needed the same cold-feet solution. They patented their design in Canada, the United States and Great Britain, and Cosysoles was born. Allan and his family ran their website business on a part-time basis for nearly ten years before coming into the Den in 2009.

Looking for an investor to help them grow, the family asked for $150,000 for 30 percent of their company. I gave them $30,000 cash in exchange for 10 percent equity, plus a $120,000 line of credit. With no debt to service, they've left their line of credit untouched. After the show, internet sales skyrocketed—a 200 percent increase in sales over prior years. Allan describes the next several months as "a crazy ride" as he was flooded with offers by potential investors, wholesalers and retailers. Allan spent a good deal of time evaluating the opportunities and eventually established a relationship with Tender Tootsies out of London, Ontario, long-time manufacturers of slippers and footwear. Tender Tootsies sells through its established network of department stores and pharmacies. We negotiated a royalty arrangement whereby they manufacture and distribute Cosysoles in Canada. Tender Tootsies has shipped Cosysoles to about 250 Canadian Walmart stores and another 333 pharmacy locations, including Drug Trading, Pharmasave, London Drugs, Pharma Plus, Rexall and Metro pharmacies. Allan continues to sell Cosysoles on the website and is also selling to hospital retailers and home health-care providers.

Unlike other products, Cosysoles are designed to allow the wearer to walk around safely and comfortably during use. Cosysoles are made to fit securely, while other products tend to be one size fits all, or they use heating-pad inserts that don't work as well, or aren't as safe.

Like most start-ups, Cosysoles has been focused on gaining exposure for their product. Some big media opportunities have come their way, such as a *Wall Street Journal* article outlining ways to save on energy bills. Tender Tooties has enhanced the Cosysoles profile through a strong retail presence and various forms of advertising. Until 2009, Allan managed the manufacturing process, but Tender Tootsies has assumed that responsibility as part of the royalty agreement, freeing Allan up to focus on other aspects of the operation.

So many people can benefit from the therapeutic benefits of Cosysoles that the founders have focused on getting their product into hospitals and long-term-care facilities. Their primary entry into these locations is through small health and wellness–related wholesalers. Allan sees lots of opportunity ahead, including the possibility of adding a designer slipper for sale in higher-end retail stores. They just need a little extra horsepower to take advantage of these new markets. Next year, they're looking forward to moving into the U.S. market, and expanding their presence in Canada. Following a solid entry into the United States, they're considering establishing a presence in Britain.

Overall, Allan is loving his entrepreneurial journey. "If you're passionate about a product, are prepared to work hard and can work with the right people, it's a lot of fun. I'm enjoying this even more than my years in the IT corporate world," he says. With a challenging and rewarding business on his hands at the age of sixty-five, Allan is redefining retirement and only looking forward. "This is my baby," he says. "I just want to keep helping it grow!"

Dr. Mist

Claudette Leduc, the entrepreneur behind Dr. Mist natural deodorant, has a fascinating backstory that never made it to air. Working as a corporate director of customer service, she was achieving significant growth for her employer. The entrepreneurial spirit emerged when she started wondering what would happen if she put her substantial talent to work in her own business. "Being older, I was afraid of the risk, but something told me I would make it," she says. As a consumer, she had been looking for a natural deodorant that was aluminum- and alum-free, but she wasn't happy with what was already on the market. Then she stumbled upon Dr. Mist, an odourless body spray made with Dead Sea minerals

"Are entrepreneurs born or made? Is it innate or can it be learned? The answer is a simple yes."—WBW

and salt that creates a powdery bacterial shield on the skin and kills bacteria. Because the bacteria can't react with the skin's sweat glands, the body remains odour-free.

The invention is brilliantly simple, and it earned the inventor the coveted medical award from the International Exhibition of Inventions in Geneva, which celebrates innovation and product excellence. When Claudette read about the product, she found it and tried it. "I was shocked," she recalls. "Three days later, it was still effective. I was blown away." Thinking she wouldn't be the only one to be impressed with the spray, she offered it to some naturopathic doctors. They loved it too. "I knew I had a winner," she says. She contacted the inventor (who lives in Malaysia) and negotiated a deal to become the North American master distributor. She placed an order for 150 master cartons—about 25,000 units—to seal the deal.

She sold her entire, much-loved collection of art deco antiques to finance her first supply of stock and lived with a bed and computer for a year. She issued a news release describing the new product to local media before she even had it in the stores. The resulting attention created a strong public response: consumers started asking—even demanding—that their retailers carry Dr. Mist. By the time she came to Dragons' Den, Claudette had already secured relationships with several national retailers, including London Drugs and Loblaws/Superstore, and generated around $250,000 in sales. She came to the Den looking for additional funding to help her expand her presence in the billion-dollar deodorant market.

Claudette asked for $100,000 for 20 percent of her company. I offered her the $100,000 but also asked for a 5 percent royalty on all sales and she accepted. During due diligence, we agreed that the royalty would apply to net sales rather than gross, which allowed Claudette to subtract operating costs from overall sales. Days after the show aired, Costco called. They wanted to test the product in ten stores. A string of new distributors followed suit. Claudette estimates that since the show aired in January 2010, around 120,000 units have sold, which, for the stores, represents nearly a million dollars in gross revenues.

Claudette admits it's been tough finding brokers to help gain a presence in the bigger pharmacy chains. Another challenge is managing the U.S. market. "Brokers in the U.S. work on large retainers," Claudette explains, "so you have to spend a lot of money up front just to get someone to agree to represent you—with no guarantee that they'll generate any sales." Claudette pays for the product two months in advance of receipt, and doesn't get the revenue back until thirty days after the product is sold, which makes cash flow a constant issue. She's also learning how to best allocate her advertising budget, a significant expense for any start-up.

A lot of Claudette's success has come through word of mouth. Two women in the United States were so crazy about the product that through their determination and persistence, they persuaded two large retailers in Colorado and Georgia to carry it. Who would turn down that kind of sales support?

Claudette has brought in two scented versions of Dr. Mist, lavender and baby powder, made with essential oils. Sales have been very strong—she even ran out of the scented products last month. Reflecting on her journey, Claudette calls going into business for herself "the best decision I ever made." Because she knows how scary it can be to take that first step, she spends much of her time mentoring other budding entrepreneurs. She's finally replaced her furniture. "I would sell it all again in a heartbeat," she says.

Earth Innovations

Back in 2004 Mark Watson watched his eight-year-old cocker spaniel, Grover, die suddenly of cancer. He then learned that cancer in pets is often linked to toxins, such as mercury and lead, in road salt, which dogs can ingest by licking their paws after winter walks.

Road salt poses a major risk not only to pets, but also to humans, municipal infrastructure, vehicles and the environment. The United States and Canada use a combined 40 million tons of road salt a year, resulting in nearly $40 billion in damage to infrastructure annually. Road salt is also the main contaminant in our water system: and once it's in the water table, it can never be removed, an issue which both my friend Robert F. Kennedy's Waterkeeper Alliance and the David Suzuki Foundation have been raising for years.

Responding to these issues, Mark co-founded Earth Innovations Inc., which is focused on finding effective non-toxic solutions to everyday problems. He tracked down a cost-effective volcanic mineral that provides good traction on ice and snow, and is safe for pets, plants and property. With a natural jagged structure that sticks into ice, the rock absorbs the layer of water that sits on top of ice, implants itself and creates a solid sandpaper-like surface. Unlike salt, EcoTraction even works in very cold temperatures and creates traction in freezing rain.

In a short time, the company went from selling EcoTraction in a dozen stores to having more than five thousand retail partners across Canada, including Home Depot, Canadian Tire and Home Hardware.

Mark came in asking for $150,000 for 5 percent of the company—a $3-million valuation. I offered $500,000 for one-third of the company—a valuation of $1.5 million. All five Dragons jumped on board. After some on-air negotiating, we all agreed on $500,000 for 25 percent of the company—a valuation of $2 million.

After five months of due diligence, and just days before closing, one of the Dragons suggested we change the terms of the deal, adding an extra 10 percent annual dividend to our investment. When Mark balked, the other Dragons walked away. I was committed to honouring the original deal, and went on to invest $250,000 for 12.5 percent.

"Until you can sell it, you have no product, and until you can sell it at a profit, you have no business."—WBW

One of the company's biggest annual challenges has been the weather. The product's sale cycle is only four months long, and three warm winters in a row will naturally affect demand. When product is linked to weather, keeping retailers well supplied is tricky, especially with retailers' growing preference for just-in-time inventory.

To stabilize the revenue stream, Mark has added two new year-round products to the company's line. EcoCompo is an all-natural aid that absorbs food odours and even traps methane gas. As more municipalities introduce green bins, managing odour and gas emissions from waste is a new and growing problem—in Ontario alone, four million households now have green bins. Mark is also preparing a version of EcoCompo for industrial use in farms and zoos. The company is also taking on the baking soda industry with EcoAir-O, an all-natural and chemical-free way to absorb a multitude of odours from fridges, recreation and other vehicles, athletic bags and storage lockers.

The volcanic rock used in Earth Innovations products has been called "the miracle mineral" and it truly is. It can even be fed to beef cattle to naturally increase their size and yield—without dangerous growth hormones. It's also a tested non-toxic solution for nuclear waste cleanup.

Mark is seeking investors to grow these new opportunities and expand the EcoTraction market. He says that going after the salt industry is a little like David going after Goliath. In addition to retail, Mark has focused on securing contracts with larger clients, such as the Toronto District School Board, which has now approved EcoTraction for use in some six hundred schools. As part of their corporate giving strategy, Earth Innovations supplies Ronald McDonald House across the country with their product.

Earth Innovations is well positioned to help over twelve thousand municipalities in the North American snowbelt turn their streets green, and is using its growing social media presence as part of its marketing platform.

Mark is extremely bullish about the future. "The next generation is incredibly green, and extremely knowledgeable," Mark says. "They're asking for these solutions." He's equally positive about the entrepreneurial experience. "It's not a cakewalk," he says, "but we're really proud of what we've accomplished."

Easy-Hitch

Anyone who has a boat trailer knows how absolutely maddening it can be trying to hook it up while backing up blind. Jack Julicher came up with an easy way to hitch a trailer to the back of a vehicle. His product, appropriately called Easy-Hitch, consists of two metal rods that simply line up in your vehicle's rear-view mirror: one goes on the towing vehicle, the other on the trailer. Jack calls it the "marriage saver, bumper saver, back saver." I called it a great idea, one that I had actually tried to find online several years before Jack showed up in the Den.

Jack conceived of Easy-Hitch back in 1992, but it took a few years to turn the idea into reality. In the late 1990s, he had a prototype built in Taiwan and ordered 3,500 units. His first distributor got Kmart to take 1,500 units. They put it in fifteen of their most popular stores and it sold out within forty-eight hours. Kmart immediately ordered another twenty thousand units. Then 9/11 hit. By the spring of 2002, Kmart was in Chapter 11, and Jack lost his inventory—and a fair bit of cash. He tried to bounce back, but was struggling with the cost of maintaining a reasonable inventory. His sister-in-law suggested he go on Dragons' Den. Jack saw the opportunity as his last kick at the can. If he didn't get a deal, he and his wife Ev were prepared to shut things down.

Jack came in asking for $60,000 for 20 percent of his company. The other Dragons quickly turned him down because of that valuation. I shared the view that the valuation was seriously off base, but I was prepared to help Jack get the cash he needed to purchase more inventory. I offered him the $60,000 in the form of an inventory loan—basically a line of credit that would operate for two years. The offer was exactly what Jack needed to keep his company afloat; he accepted.

Soon after the show aired, Jack sold $15,000 worth of product on the Dragons' Den website alone. He has since sold the $60,000 worth of inventory I funded and has another $75,000 worth of product in his basement. He fully repaid my two-year loan within twenty months: I fondly remember his pride when we spoke after he paid it off.

In total, Jack and Easy-Hitch earned $80,000 in revenue between 2001 and 2009. After his Dragons' Den appearance, he generated $70,000 in revenue in 2010 and another $75,000 in 2011.

Jack still works full-time as an electrician at General Motors in Oshawa. He puts in another hour per day on Easy-Hitch. Princess Auto has been his best customer to date but it's been tough getting through to retail buyers because he simply doesn't have the right connections. The state of the economy, particularly in the United States, also doesn't help. Even with all the ups and downs, Jack is positive about the entrepreneurial experience. "You've got to have a bit of luck," he says. "We were very lucky to get on Dragons' Den and to have Brett loan us some money. We're on the edge of success now and just need a little more luck."

In addition to retail sales, Jack has also focused on growing online sales, particularly through his own website and others like www.etrailer.com. Because he lacks connections, he's in the process of hiring someone who can introduce him to the best buyers, who can then help him boost his retail presence.

Jack suffers from Parkinson's but says his health is good and his quality of life is great. He's optimistic about the future, but he's also realistic. "You can have success one minute and be gone the next. But my advice is to never give up. Especially if you think you're doing something that's for the good of others."

Frogbox

Frogbox's brilliantly simple concept is to provide convenient, cost-effective and environmentally friendly plastic moving boxes as an alternative to cardboard. Focused on protecting the environment and relieving stress for the 5.5 million Canadians who move each year, Frogbox had already attracted a piece of the billion-dollar market before entering the Den. It was also hands-down one of the most sound and well-structured companies to ever make a pitch. Strong business fundamentals, combined with a strong marketing platform, earned

> "When I thought I couldn't go on, I forced myself to keep going. My success is based on persistence, not luck."—Estée Lauder

Frogbox three competing offers from all five Dragons. After a fair amount of haggling, Doug settled on a deal with me, Jim and Arlene at $200k for 25 percent equity.

Doug describes the due diligence process as "rigorous," but it proved that his numbers were accurate, which only enhanced his already high level of credibility and trustworthiness. It was obvious that Jim and I could build a strong business relationship with Doug based on compatible values. Arlene made her investment conditional on the exclusive use of Venture Communications for all of Frogbox's marketing work. Doug wouldn't agree to exclusivity and Arlene logically pulled out of the deal.

Doug is a passionate entrepreneur who knows his business, the industry and the potential market. As a business, Frogbox just makes sense: it's easy to explain and has strong potential for growth—excellent fundamentals for any start-up. One of Doug's first challenges was to decide whether to franchise or grow through corporate expansion. Following the show, he ramped up his efforts to systemize the business and finally felt that he had a strong service model for customers and a profitable franchise model for franchisees. Doug had thousands of requests from franchisees even before the show aired. His appearance on the Den attracted many more.

> "Remember that not getting what you want is sometimes a wonderful stroke of luck."
> —Dalai Lama

Before appearing in the Den, Doug operated from three locations (two in Canada one in the United States). A mere six months later, Frogbox operated in nineteen locations: sixteen in Canada, including fifteen franchises (Vancouver is corporate); and one corporate location in each of Seattle and Minneapolis. He recently sold his first U.S. franchise in Boise, Idaho.

Frogbox is a relatively low-cost franchise. At $10,000 to $30,000 based on population size, plus trucks, boxes and marketing costs, the buy-in price is low because there's no need for a huge real-estate investment. Doug says the biggest surprise following his Den appearance was how many qualified people applied for franchises, and how many were from the United States.

Getting all those people up and running is a big challenge. Although Frogbox is a simple concept, running the business properly—and profitably—is fairly complex. It requires not just a strong marketing mix, but also efficient scheduling and routing systems that allow each franchise to operate at scale. Doug's focus has been on solidifying and simplifying the branding message and creating an operations manual to make the business turnkey for each new franchisee.

Doug admits there are plenty of mom-and-pop start-ups trying to compete with Frogbox, but maintains that it's harder for small operators to provide proper customer service. The cost of renting boxes is about the same as purchasing cardboard boxes and includes pickup and delivery. Since Frogbox is about selling convenience and relieving the stress of moving, expansion only increases the convenience factor for clients because Frogbox boxes can now move around from centre to centre. "As we expand, we have the ability to move people from anywhere to anywhere," Doug says.

"It's been more work than I could possibly imagine. This opportunity was more than I could have hoped for and will probably never come again in my lifetime. Our stretch goal was for ten franchises in 2011 and we hit nineteen halfway through the year. Growth is limited by how well you can find great partners. We've grown quickly because we've been able to attract high-calibre people quickly."

Doug estimates that Frogbox will be in the fifty biggest U.S. cities over a two- to three-year period. Within Canada, Frogbox will roll out to smaller cities like Kingston and Barrie and others over the same time frame.

Hillberg & Berk

Rachel Mielke is a Regina-based jewellery designer and the first deal I ever did in the Den. Maybe it was her Saskatchewan roots, maybe it was her swagger (a combination of business savvy and self-belief) that made me say, "I'm in." Either way, I'm enormously glad I did. People don't often associate Saskatchewan with high fashion, but Rachel is changing that attitude as H&B establishes its name in the Canadian jewellery industry.

Rachel actually made two pitches to the Dragons, not one. She came into the Den with a strong presentation, but all five of us had trouble coming to terms with her company valuation—around $300,000 for 20 percent of the company. The valuation was based on future projections, but she only had a year or so of sales revenues behind her. Her first pitch failed, but the producers were so impressed by the product and with my encouragement and Rachel's entrepreneurial spirit that they asked her to pitch again. She came back later that day, this time asking for $200,000 for 20 percent of the company. I countered with an offer of $200,000 for 30 percent and she accepted. We had a deal.

Dragons' Den is tricky. Even though only six or seven minutes make it to air, the actual pitches can take between twenty and ninety minutes. During that time, the Dragons have to figure out the business, the market, the skill and knowledge of the entrepreneur, and decide on a fair valuation—not an easy thing to do in a short time frame. I look at the numbers, but I also go by gut instinct. The quality of Rachel's product was unquestionable. She also knew her market, and wasn't afraid to go head-to-head with Kevin when he pressed her on the potential of her company. She clearly understood marketing and her business skill was obvious. In the end, everything added up. She was young and untested, but something told me Rachel was worth my time and money. As I said on the show, "I'm willing to invest in *you*."

There were no surprises with Rachel. The deal we made on air is the deal we signed. Although there was a bit of delay at the outset, she did hit her aggressive projections and has continued to do so every year since.

"Starting out in Saskatchewan in an unlikely industry hasn't been easy," says Rachel. "Having no mentors, I had to learn everything from scratch. I made a lot of mistakes, but they taught me valuable lessons and got me where I am now. I still struggle with feeling like an outsider in Canada's fashion industry. Since my brand is not well known on either end of Canada, we have to work very hard to open doors. Despite Brett's demanding career, he regularly takes the time to discuss the growth of H&B, and I believe he treats me with the same respect he would his biggest investment partner. From the beginning, my philosophy has been about creating social change for women. I'm doing more than encouraging them to invest in beautiful, wearable jewellery; I'm also encouraging them to believe in and invest in themselves. Brett has shown me that social opportunity not only has a place in business—it is the new movement in business. As my brand becomes more recognized, and our sales break records for many of the stores that carry it, I'm getting closer to realizing my dream of having the top designer jewellery brand in Canada."

Aside from business guidance, what I have been able to offer Rachel is a bigger platform for establishing her brand. Her designs are now worn by some of the most beautiful and famous women in the world. Since we signed, Rachel has taken her modest company from $100,000 in sales to over $1.5 million in just three years. And she's done it all while staying put in Regina—the home that she loves.

Karoleena

Kurt and Kris Goodjohn came to the Den pitching their high-end modular building company, Karoleena Inc. The brothers were taking on the traditional "stick build" construction process and finding a niche to compete with long-established inner-city builders. Modular homes are constructed off-site in a matter of a month or two and craned together on-site in less than a day, taking much of the frustration, uncertainty and risk out of the construction process. With an eye for designs that feature state-of-the-art energy-efficient technologies and forward-thinking materials and finishes, Karoleena Inc. is making prefab home construction "pretty fabulous."

The brothers had a great concept but they had run into cash flow problems that meant they needed funds to help them manage their debt load and expand their operations. They asked for $500,000 for 25 percent of the company. They got $250,000 for 10 percent and an operating line for the balance.

During due diligence, my team and I had more than a few marathon sessions with Kurt and Kris to determine how we could best work together. My initial role was to provide a loan to help with cash flow, which was later converted into equity. During the due diligence process, other investors bought into the company, which allowed Karoleena to set up their own factory. Rather than subcontracting everything out, they were able to gain control over production, which took a lot of the risk out of the process and allowed for exponential growth.

One challenge for Karoleena is to dispel some of the myths about modular construction. The advantages are obvious: the optimal building season lasts all year long and since 95 percent of the build happens in a controlled manufacturing facility, there is no exposure to the elements. Another challenge the brothers found was that the inner-city builder's market is crowded and hard to crack. They have since taken the modular concept to rural recreational opportunities, where cabin/cottage owners can take advantage of the modular building process and ship a unit to a rural location and have a home in a weekend.

While virtually any home can be designed (i.e., customized) using Karoleena's system, they are focusing on selling pre-existing designs for single- and multi-family homes, cabins and office spaces. It can be tempting to want to create a dream home (or office) from scratch, but the process can be prohibitively expensive—and intimidating. Karoleena offers increased certainty: people know exactly how long the build will take, with no delays caused by weather or missed deadlines. They also know exactly what the end result will look like, which equals less stress, fewer speed bumps and no need to supervise construction—which is especially appealing to people in the recreation property market, who often can't be on-site because of its distant location.

During their early years, Karoleena's annual revenues were between $1 million and $2 million a year. With the evolution of the business to encompass rural recreation homes, their order book has grown to almost $20 million. As they grow, their biggest challenge is managing the production process. Until about a year ago, their team consisted of just the two of them. They've always had to manage tradespeople, but now they have employees—ten full-time people in the office and up to thirty on the shop floor. The big lesson: how important it is to have good people around them. They want people with passion and personalities that align with their own. They're finding out—sometimes the hard way—that trusting your gut is the most important part of the hiring process.

"Coming into the Den, we didn't just want money, we wanted expertise—which is invaluable. Brett gave us his time and energy, and exposed us to the possibilities of what we could do," says Kurt. Kurt and Kris feel fortunate to be on the upswing of their business. They've worked hard, so they don't consider themselves lucky, but are enormously grateful for where they are. On the brink of disaster only a few years ago, Kurt found himself living in his parents' basement, and both brothers worked at part-time jobs to make ends meet. They don't consider any challenge they face now to be as tough as those humbling early years.

"Perseverance is the biggest thing," says Kurt. "We could have given up at any time, but we believed in what we were doing. Most partnerships would have fallen apart by now. But we're brothers. We've shared the ups and downs and we'll hopefully prosper together."

Kelvin Tools

When Kevin Royes came into the Den, Debbie Travis, the Renovation Queen, was on the panel as a celebrity Dragon. Kevin had one cool tool—the Kelvin.23 all-in-one—which integrates twenty-three essential tools, including a hammer, level and screwdrivers, into a single device. Debbie called it the Swiss Army knife of home decoration. While we were all keen on the investment, it was Jim, Arlene and Robert who got the final deal. However, I said to Kevin before he left the Den, "If these Dragons don't close or the deal doesn't work out, call me."

The original deal was $500,000 for 25 percent equity, but it derailed during due diligence. A partner in China had a contractual dispute with the company that restricted Kevin from taking on new investors. The whole thing fell apart. When I heard that the deal had fallen through, nearly a year after filming, Kevin and I reconnected. We struck and closed a deal in a few months, based on a lower corporate valuation. I assumed the deal at $250,000 for 25 percent equity, plus a $300,000 loan. We didn't agree with the original valuation because Kevin's sales hadn't hit the projections he'd made the year before. We had to restructure the company, and part of the cash was used to pay out the partner in China. The loan also allowed him to finance inventory and purchase new production moulds.

Kevin calls himself an "inventor-preneur" and he has one of the most creative and clever minds I've ever come across. I also love the tool. It's a brilliant idea that works well and looks great. In my mind, it belongs in everyone's boat, car and kitchen drawer, and it's the perfect wedding or Father's Day gift.

Manufacturing is a constant challenge. Finding a factory that provides a good-quality product with reasonable margins is tough. Kevin's now working with his fourth factory in two years, and he's getting moulds to a fifth. The supply chain always seems to take longer than anticipated. If the product is late, he misses filling sales orders. In one case, he had to airfreight product to a retailer, an expense that ate his margins, but kept the customer happy. Contractual penalty clauses are one way to deal with late suppliers. But at the end of the day, when a supplier doesn't come through, it's not the supplier's problem—it's yours.

Sales are another challenge. This is a new category of tool that doesn't easily fit in the market. When the Leatherman Multi-Tool came out, no one knew where it belonged. The Kelvin.23 is similar. It doesn't really belong with the hard-core tools in Home Depot. It's more of a light-to-medium tool that is better suited to housewares or home decor. It's also starting to take off in gift departments. In large part, Kevin's had to continually clarify what business he's really in. And if he strikes out with the tool buyers during one buying cycle, it could take several months before he can speak to buyers from other departments, which affects his cash flow.

Marketing is another challenge. There is a lot of potential going the infomercial route, and Kevin has looked aggressively at this option. The problem is that while infomercials could drive significant sales, his production cycle isn't yet reliable enough to respond to that kind of demand. With the right marketing approach, Kevin could be selling 20,000 units a month, but so far his manufacturing ability can only handle about 50,000 units per year.

Since signing, Kevin has generated significant interest in his product and secured retail partners including Canadian Tire and Home Depot. He has purchase orders for thousands of units. But he's still trying to solidify a manufacturing relationship that will let him reliably meet and grow his sales projections. Kevin is pragmatic about all the frustrations: "Entrepreneurs are problem solvers. We have to be comfortable with a certain amount of uncertainty. This is what I'll do for the rest of my life. But sometimes I wonder if it has to be so hard."

We have made a good return off of the Kelvin.23 since I invested, but Kevin is struggling now with the challenge of being a single-product company, and is working hard to either expand his product offerings or find another approach to the market with just one great product.

MacKenzie and Marr Guitars

When they came to Dragons' Den, John Marr and Jonathan MacKenzie wanted help manufacturing what they predicted would be a winning product: handcrafted, solid wood acoustic guitars made in China. But their sales model had a twist. They were going to retail the guitar strictly over the internet. The pair had a factory in China whose highly skilled workers could produce guitars of exceptional quality. By focusing on online sales, they could significantly reduce overhead, and offer a high-end guitar at a fraction of the cost of the competition. As part of the pitch, John and Jonathan invited talented hobby guitarist Kevin O'Leary to try their prototype. They brought along a $5,000 guitar and dared a blindfolded Kevin to tell the difference between the $900 prototype and the more expensive model. Kevin picked the MacKenzie and Marr as the better, more expensive guitar. For Kevin, Jim and me, their pitch was—as the saying goes—music to our ears, and we immediately cut a deal.

With zero sales, John and Jonathan based their valuation on a cash flow analysis, asking for enough money to place the first order and maintain a positive cash flow for the first year. The three of us took a 15 percent equity stake for $15,000 and loaned another $20,000 in return for a small royalty on retail sales for the term of the debt.

"When I invest, I look for people who are committed. I don't need to know their business, but I need to know that they really know their business."—WBW

Language and cultural barriers inherent in dealing with a factory halfway around the world have been the biggest obstacles for John and Jonathan. They're producing an intricate, handmade instrument, and details can easily get lost in translation. Changes in size, bracing, shape or wood can result in a dramatically different instrument. The pair fine-tuned the design for some six months when they first began, varying the details until they got the sound they were looking for. They then took their prototype to an Ottawa-area guitar store and played it against every guitar there—that's when they knew they could outperform the more expensive competition.

Their episode aired about eight months after the pitch. During that time, they started to build their inventory. The show produced a flood of orders. Eighteen hours later, John and Jonathan had sold all forty-eight guitars in inventory. Orders kept coming in, but the factory was stalled—and more guitars weren't being made. After multiple trips to China, countless emails and dozens of Skype calls, John eventually got production back on track. It took a full eighteen months before the production and delivery system was solid. Even with all the frustration and delays, they didn't lose a single order. Customers were willing to wait—some more patiently than others— and have been delighted with their new guitars. John describes the glowing feedback as "almost embarrassing."

"This isn't amateur hour," says John. "Brett's so perceptive, it's spooky. He understands exactly what we're doing and immediately zeroes in on what's working and what isn't. That's what I appreciate in a partner." Through the process, John has learned a lot about making decisions and living with them. "There's a time for gathering information, and a time for making choices. Once you've made that choice, you have to learn to live with the results," he says. John and Jonathan have also adopted a strategy for giving back. They recently began donating $100 for every guitar sold in a given promotion to a Montreal charity, Dans la Rue, that reaches out to street kids.

John and Jonathan are creating a series of guitars that pay tribute to some of the finest acoustic performers of our time. The first was a limited edition guitar named for legendary folk and country singer Ian Tyson. More recently they came to an agreement with an American singer of the same vintage as Tyson, Tom Rush. Now that they have a reliable manufacturing process, they'll be launching the new signature guitar, priced at $2,000 and comparable to much more expensive guitars, with emphasis on the full North American market.

MacKenzie and Marr's first year of sales was a modest $100,000, but they're projecting between $250,000 and $300,000 for the current year. If all goes well with the U.S. launch, John believes sales could reach $2 million. "Without sounding arrogant, we think we might have the best guitar for the money in the world," he says.

Modrobes

One of the most interesting entrepreneurs to pitch in the Den is Steven Sal Debus, who started a version of his company—Modrobes—right out of university. His concept, stylish environment-friendly clothing, generated $70,000 in revenue in its first year. By year four, he was up to $10 million. But he chose the wrong group of partners to help him run the company and they apparently ran it into the ground.

When Steven took the company back, Modrobes was nearly bankrupt. Scaling back and reducing costs helped him get back on course. It took nearly three years to get Modrobes running free and clear again. During that time, Steven was inspired to research environmentally sustainable fabric options. New technology made it possible for a developer like Steven to make lightweight cotton-like fabrics out of recycled pop bottles. In addition, Steven discovered how to make his own trademarked fabric out of eucalyptus trees. The product, Eucalyptex, is an odour-resistant, quick-drying, hypoallergenic, comfortable fabric that easily outperforms wool or polyester.

Next, Steven took another innovative step. He opened a retail store on Toronto's Queen Street that functioned as a test laboratory, letting Steven test his designs with immediate street-level feedback. While Modrobes had previously attracted fashion *and* sport customers, his new customers were solid sport enthusiasts. Based on this experience, he built a product line, shut down the store and focused on the wholesale market, targeting running, yoga, outdoor and cycling stores. The wholesale focus helped him build a more solid foundation for the company, keeping his overhead low and allowing him to develop a very focused product line.

By 2010, an updated, sustainable and environmentally friendly version of Modrobes was reborn. In order to effectively re-launch the company, Steven was looking for investors to help get his production processes in place.

Steven asked for $200,000 for 20 percent of the company. He got offers from both Jim and Kevin, but turned them down because they were looking for 50 percent or more—more than he felt comfortable giving up. I offered him a $100,000 equity investment and $100,000 line of credit for 25 percent, which he took. After due diligence, during which we discovered that his previous revenues were exactly what he said they were, I topped up another $30,000 to the equity investment and operating line.

Being a manufacturer of both fabric and clothing adds a layer of complexity to Steven's business. Manufacturing the fabric can add two months to production schedules. Once he's paid for the fabric and manufacturing, and ships the product, he still has to wait sixty-to-eighty days before getting paid by the retailer, making cash flow calculations tricky.

Steven has upwards of one hundred wholesale accounts in the United States, Canada, Europe, Australia and New Zealand, secured mostly through trade and consumer shows, and enthusiastic customers promoting the product through word of mouth. While he's seeing growth, Steven still finds the current economic climate difficult. "This is not a growth economy," he says. "Because there's less disposable income, lots of stores are shrinking their product offerings. They want to focus on what's working, which can make it harder to get them to pick up a new product line."

Fortunately, Steven's product is standing out from the crowd, enabling him to generate between $300,000 and $400,000 in sales this year.

"Brett takes a relatively hands-off approach to investing, which I appreciate," Steven says. "I like that he's there as a mentor and advisor, but he's not in my face. In my experience, a lot of entrepreneurs are psychotic, stubborn egomaniacs—myself included. So his approach works for me. I wouldn't be here without him. We need more nice-guy investors like Brett in the business world. He proves that you don't have to be an asshole to be good at business."

Steven is focused on hitting more trade and consumer shows over the next year to help boost his distribution channels. Over the next decade, he hopes to grow his wholesale network to include upwards of one thousand suppliers, with revenues in the $50-to-$100-million category.

Steve is now facing challenges in terms of funding growth: he wants to add products and inventory to his offering in advance of sales growth, which is the classic entrepreneurial dilemma. He says he is up for the challenge.

Moxie Trades

Moxie Trades is the home of the original pink workboot for women, and the brainchild of Marissa McTasney, who happens to be *full* of moxie. As a woman working in construction, Marissa needed boots to keep her safe on the job. Being fashion-conscious, she went looking for pink steel-toed boots, but couldn't find any. She quickly saw an opportunity to cater to the growing number of women working in trades. Moxie Trades products are designed for women, by women, combining the best of comfort, safety, design and fashion.

Before Marissa came into the Den, she already had business and retail partners, and strong sales. She was a confident presenter who knew the value of her business. In real time, her pitch was 2.5 hours (the longest in Den history to my knowledge), and one of the most interesting negotiations ever in the Den. On air, Robert and I offered $600,000 for 75 percent of the business. It was an animated discussion that hinged on the valuation. Given the strength of her sales, Jim told her not to take the deal. She listened and turned us down. No hard feelings, we hugged and as she left the Den, I issued the offer of assistance quoted in a previous chapter. That night, she called.

She knew that dealing with partners like Mark's Work Wearhouse, Walmart and Zellers would require a larger investor to help manage inventory and logistics. We had breakfast the next day and shook on a deal. I bought 50 percent of the company from another shareholder with a combination of cash and shareholder loans totalling $600,000. Marissa has fantastic energy and natural sales ability. Her moxie, passion and business sense had me from "Hello, Dragons."

By 2008, after two years in business, Moxie Trades had $1 million in gross revenue. Then 2009 hit. Marissa found out how difficult it can be for a start-up to provide the best marketing, price and customer service to the large retailers. Fines for late inventory can kill a small business. Logistics to support supply are critical. At the time, she was doing it all herself. She lost Walmart and Zellers. Her biggest clients became her biggest competitors, selling their own line of workwear for women. Devastated, she had to start all over again.

"Being able to sell yourself and your ideas is as fundamental to business as understanding the value of a brand, knowing how to build goodwill with clients, and the importance of product differentiation."—WBW

After losing her biggest retailers, she thought she was done. We encouraged her to stay the course. She revamped the product line, hired staff and pre-booked sales: she didn't put anything into production until the sales were booked. That worked so well that in 2010 she ran out of inventory. She went from $150,000 in 2009 to $1.5 million in 2010. She was still having trouble forecasting sales, so she partnered with a distribution company to take over logistics and inventory. They'd worry about bringing in the product from China, delivery and accounts payable, and pay Moxie Trades a commission in the form of a royalty. Using a distributor has freed Marissa up to do what she's really good at: sales and marketing, and managing her main accounts, including a strong relationship with one of Canada's largest retailers, Mark's Work Wearhouse, which now carries her products in 130 stores nationwide.

"I was prepared to walk away from my company in 2009," Marissa says, "but Brett believed in me more than I believed in myself. Working with a distribution company really saved me. I resisted it at first. I wanted success on my terms. But Brett saw that I was only getting three to four hours' sleep a night. He said, 'I'm scared you're going to get divorced and kill yourself.' Using a distributorship forced me to lay off staff, which was hard. Then I read a book called *Double Double* by Cameron Herold that talked about creating a dynasty with zero full-time staff. It gave me a new vision. Now I've embraced my new reality. I could still work twenty-four hours a day, but I don't have to. I can have dinner with my kids every night. I'm a better wife and mother now. My company just hit the five-year mark. I've learned so much, and I'm proud that I've survived this long and have built something strong and stable. It's just about growing now. My original loan from the Business Development Corporation is almost paid off and my personal liability is going down, which feels great. Brett's shareholder loans grew way beyond his original commitment and, thankfully, he's patient and believes in me. I hope that one day I can make him proud and give him *all* his money back. In the past five years, I've also found a platform for giving back. I volunteer my time and raise money for Habitat for Humanity as an ambassador. As great as it is to be a receiver, giving is even better."

Marissa still has her ups and downs, but she's learned a lot about the cyclical nature of the footwear industry. She has six regional reps in Canada and four in the United States who market to retailers and end users. With regional reps in place, it's just about building. She's discovered that working with independent retailers, such as privately owned safety stores, is a more reliable business model because their needs are easier to meet. She's working on building a network of suppliers across North America so that if she loses one, it won't cost her the entire business.

Pro Elvis Jumpsuits

Eleanor von Boetticher is a trained costumer who began her career working in theatre. An out-of-the-blue call from an Elvis tribute artist, Will Reeb, changed her business path. He asked if she would consider making costumes for him and for other tribute artists. Eleanor continued to work full-time in theatre and film, while Will looked after the customer relationships and Eleanor sewed the costumes. Without much marketing or effort, the customers started coming in. Surprised? Consider that there are some eighty thousand Elvis impersonators worldwide, each of whom owns an average of three costumes. Some, especially those who tour all year and put on three or four shows a week, have as many as ten or twelve costumes.

Eleanor was looking for a way to work from home and start a family. So in 2007, she took over the business from Will and Pro Elvis Jumpsuits was born. From 2007 to 2009, working part-time with two small children, Eleanor generated about $10,000 in sales each year.

She began to notice that the Elvis costume market was geared towards custom orders that would take three to four months to fill. She realized that offering mid- to high-end costumes off the rack could greatly boost sales, but she needed extra capital to create a solid costume inventory.

Eleanor came into the Den asking for $30,000 for a 30 percent stake in her company. All of the Dragons loved the concept. Even though it was a small company with relatively limited potential, Eleanor showed that she had a very good handle on her market and knew where the opportunities were. I gave her a $25,000 line of credit and paid $5,000 for a 5 percent net profit participation to give her the $30,000.

Eleanor's average costume costs around $1,000, with a range of $500 to almost $4,000. She runs a basement workshop with seven part-time workers. Having flexible shop hours and allowing employees to work from home has helped her attract highly skilled workers.

But it can take from ten to over one hundred hours to make one costume, so her main challenge has been developing a production system that allows her to delegate the work effectively. A part-time IT person is working to improve communication and processes among employees.

Eleanor has maintained a custom line in addition to developing a ready-to-wear line. She's still building an inventory, with the goal of having a full size-range in each of the eight styles she offers.

The other imperative has been developing systems for gathering as much information on each customer as possible. "The key for any online retailer is to develop trust. The better you know your customers and meet their needs, the more they will trust you," she explains. "If they don't trust you, they won't buy. Half of my day is spent communicating with customers. If I don't return calls and emails immediately, there's a good chance I'll lose the sale."

Like any new entrepreneur, Eleanor is learning how to keep all the balls in the air and still move forward. She's focused on constantly improving the product for fit and durability, and increasing sales.

"Brett's a great booster. His main advice has been about making sure our customers are always happy. That's a big factor in our success. For many customers, it's their first experience of being really happy from start to finish—especially when they get their costumes within a week or two instead of three to four months."

Since the show aired, sales have grown steadily upward. Sales for 2011 were $150,000 and Eleanor is projecting revenues for 2012 of $250,000 as she broadens her product line and continues to expand her customer base. She's enhancing her online marketing, including posting more videos on YouTube to guide customers on fit and measuring techniques. Because word of mouth travels fast in the tightly knit Elvis community, she'll continue to attend Elvis conventions and festivals, including Ontario's Collingwood Elvis Festival, the world's largest. While maintaining her presence in Australia, Great Britain and the United States, she's trying to expand further into the large markets of Japan and Germany. She has brought multilingual employees into the company to help with international sales. "It's a constant juggling act," she says, "but I love it."

QuickSnap

QuickSnap is a durable plastic clip that fits any laced shoe or boot. Once fastened, QuickSnap gives a consistent and comfortable tension, making it easy to snap—rather than tie—laces and go. The snaps fits any lace-able shoe, from kids' running shoes and adult dress shoes to workboots, making them particularly useful for anyone who has difficulty with laces, or for workers who need to quickly lace up a pair of boots on the job and not worry about loose laces becoming a safety hazard.

The QuickSnap founders came into the Den asking $125,000 for 20 percent of the company. Arlene and Robert offered them $125,000 for 50 percent, which was accepted. When I became aware of the military advantages of the clips, I offered to buy three sets for all of our Canadian troops serving overseas, particularly in Afghanistan. My $30,000 donation was very well received. Even the U.S. military came back asking how they could get their hands on the product.

After due diligence and for his own reasons, Robert pulled out a week before closing. I was invited by the president, Riad Byne, to invest and didn't hesitate. We closed the deal in fall 2008. I now own about $62,000 of common equity in the company. Since then, QuickSnap Inc. has established relationships with various independent Canadian stores, and in 2010 they closed their biggest deal, with Walmart. They soon began selling in eighty stores nationwide. After moving more than 70 percent of their product during the first fourteen weeks, Walmart added another eighty stores, doubling the company's Walmart presence to 160 stores across Canada. They also have relationships with SportChek and Sport Mart and are discussing the possibility of adding NHL logos to the product to expand the hockey market.

To date, the company's biggest focus has been on establishing a strong retail presence. Online sales offer a steady source of revenue, but a strong retail presence helps close the sale (people can see and touch the product), and big stores lend credibility to a start-up. But it can take a long time to turn an initial contact into product on the shelves.

Before Dragons' Den, the company had sold fewer than four hundred units. After the show, they were up to four thousand units. They re-engineered the product, and the new design and retail strategy have helped build sales of nearly four hundred thousand units. The snaps retail for six to seven dollars per pair, and word of mouth is the company's strongest marketing tool.

The dramatic 1,000 percent increase in the first year made forecasting—and financing—the manufacturing process from quarter to quarter a challenge. The company carries a working inventory for smaller stores, but most large orders take six to eight weeks to deliver. As a result, they are not always as prepared as they'd like to be to respond to increasing demand.

Time is another major challenge. Founders Drew McKenna and Riad Byne have been the company's mainstay partners. They both maintain full-time jobs and run QuickSnap on the side, sometimes pulling twenty-hour days.

The company has established a retail presence in the United States through a few independent stores, but they're focusing on boosting their sales numbers in Canada before making a concerted U.S. effort. They also want to launch two new products under their name, including a sneaker ball–deodorizer and another lace concept for children's footwear. These should be easy add-ons in an industry in which they're already established. They've also got a few new inventions in mind that they're not ready to disclose until later next year.

Both Riad and Drew have several more years before they retire from their full-time jobs. Riad wants to put in his full twenty years in the military before transitioning full-time to QuickSnap Inc. "We intend to keep going full force with QuickSnap," he says. "This is a company with a long shelf life."

Snappy Socks

One of the first questions I ask people looking for an equity investor is: How much time and money have you invested yourself? The answer usually reflects the entrepreneur's commitment. Corla Rokochy may go down in history as the most successful Den entrepreneur with the lowest initial cash investment. She auditioned with a simple $5 proto-type—a pair of socks attached with a couple of snaps. As a busy mom of five children, she has come up with a very simple but smart idea: making socks that snap together before washing and drying to make sorting, well, a snap. After the audition, Corla spent a fair amount of time registering and trademarking Snappy Socks, and creating an online presence, but she came into the Den with no sales and only a dozen or so sample socks. Since her idea made perfect sense, she still got two offers: a low-ball from Kevin (which she graciously and intelligently declined) and a joint offer from Arlene and me, which she accepted.

During due diligence and for her own reasons, Arlene decided not to proceed, but I took my 25 percent for $25,000. Corla also invested funds from her own pocket. To get the manufacturing process underway, my first priority was to get Corla connected with a China-based sourcing company, a group of Canadians who live and work in China and act as agents for Canadian entrepreneurs. One of the biggest issues was finding a snap that wouldn't rust in the wash or irritate the wearer. Once she found that, she was on her way.

Corla spent the entire $25,000 equity investment on inventory. It was six months before she had the first shipment, and she's been actively selling only since August 2011. Based largely on her Dragons' Den appearance, she has established sales relationships with fifty-five retailers located in every province in Canada and is adding two to three more stores each week. So far, she's already generated more than $20,000 in retail sales.

Corla has been a business owner before, but importing and manufacturing present a whole new learning curve. Corla has hired a sales rep to help with shipping/receiving and invoicing. "Everything takes *way* more time and money than I imagined," she admits. After three months, she was halfway through her stock, and is currently planning the timing and quantity of the next shipment, another challenge since it will take three months for the shipment to arrive, and she doesn't want to miss a potential upswing in sales, or sit on a big shipment if sales are slow.

Corla joined our group of mostly family, friends and staff who went to Mexico to build homes for the homeless. She became inspired by the opportunities for giving back, and is asking herself what more she can do to make her community a better place. "It's not just about making money," she says. Corla is philosophical about the entrepreneurial process. "When people see the socks, they say, 'why didn't I think of that?' A lot people have good ideas, but they don't follow through on them. If I've learned anything through this process, it's that if you've got an idea, go for it. You'll never regret action, but you might well regret not following your dream."

Corla capitalized on the huge Las Vegas trade show in February 2012 where eighty countries were represented. She's also in conversation with a major distribution company whose network includes 1,700 retailers, an opportunity that came from a Dragons' Den update show. As she goes into the States, she'll be looking for guidance on financing and managing inventory. If the distributor relationship develops, Corla could be looking at upwards of $250,000 in annual sales.

"Snappy Socks is one way for me to be home with my kids and generate a good income," Corla says. "I'm in it for the long-term potential. I thought going to Dragons' Den would be a fun Griswold vacation," she adds, in a reference to the 1989 film *Christmas Vacation*, which traces a family's disastrous holiday adventure. "But it's been an amazing journey."

Soap Nuts

Ever hear of soap nuts? Neither had I until Matt and Erin Johnson from Melfort, Saskatchewan, walked into the Den. They had been importing soap nuts—natural soapberries—from South Asia since 2007, and selling them locally and online. Soap nuts work the same way as any detergent, except that they're biodegradable, non-toxic, non-allergenic and antimicrobial. During the taping of the Dragons' Den episode on which they appeared, Kevin O'Leary joked, "Who knew soap nuts could save the world?" Given the enormous need for green alternatives to toxic detergents, maybe they can help solve a key environmental problem—detergent wastes.

Erin stumbled upon soap nuts when she was trying to find a way to get rid of lingering odours in their baby's cloth diapers. She was surprised at how well they worked—even better than the commercial detergents she'd tried. Another bonus: the natural detergent was so gentle that Matt no longer had eczema—a scaly, itchy rash, probably aggravated by harsher commercial detergents—after they started using them.

Erin was already selling cloth diapers in the local farmers' market, so they decided to sell soap nuts, too. They were moving well, so the couple decided to move to online sales. Ironically, Matt and Erin—who don't own a television—had never even heard of Dragons' Den, but they were encouraged to audition by friends. Because they were self-financing, they were struggling with the cost of maintaining a reasonable inventory. They came to the Den to find financial support, boost their business profile and gain a mentor. They got all three.

Matt and Erin asked for $20,000 in exchange for 30 percent of their company. The business had steadily grown from about $20,000 in the first few years, to just over $50,000 in the last couple. Their valuation was fair given growth prospects, so I gave them exactly what they were asking for.

After airing, they began receiving hundreds of orders a day. As wholesalers, they established a relationship with some one hundred private health-food suppliers and online stores throughout North America. Last year, their sales climbed to a healthy $140,000. They estimate they'll do $300,000 in sales this year.

Another bonus has been media attention, with features in *Prevention*, *Family Circle*, and *Hobby Farms* magazines. They've also been contacted by the Oprah Winfrey Network's "Buy.o.Logic" show, where soap nuts will be tested against three to four other detergents. When one of their competitors recently went out of business, Matt and Erin acquired his recipe for creating liquid soap. They're now close to selling as much liquid detergent as soap nuts. They're also jumping through the necessary hoops to certify the liquid organic, and then develop a complete line of products from shampoo and hand soap to dishwashing liquid and window cleaner.

Like many entrepreneurs, Matt says his biggest challenge is time. Because their company revenue isn't enough to replace Matt's income, he still works at a full-time job. They've hired a commissioned sales person to help out. To gain a stronger retail presence, Matt and Erin have been designing new bilingual packaging. Once they have that in place, they're looking forward to closing deals with major retailers, such as Co-op and Loblaws, and expect their business to grow enough to let Matt work on it full-time. They also have set their sights on international markets. They're in the process of getting products into South Korea through an exclusive distributor there. They think it's just a matter of time, infrastructure and packaging before they can expand worldwide.

"I'm an entrepreneur at heart," says Matt. "I'm hooked on the whole process. I see the vision of what this business can become. I love it!"

UNO and Shredder

The summer before his last year in high school in Milton, Ontario, Ben Gulak went to China with his parents. He was shocked by the transportation challenges facing China's high-density population. "*An*

Inconvenient Truth [a documentary film] had just come out. News stories about the impact of global warming were everywhere. And 100,000 new cars were hitting roadways in China every day," Ben recalls.

Ben came home inspired to create a clean and compact vehicle. He knew that in order to be marketable, green vehicles also needed to be cool. "Cars and vehicles are style statements—they're social statements," says Ben. "So I set out to create a cooler electric vehicle." He decided to merge the sex appeal of a motorcyle with the technology of a Segway. He created the Uno, a motorized unicycle that accelerates when the rider leans forward and has a control system that automatically keeps the rider balanced.

"Once I've agreed on a deal, I'll look for ways to move forward and solve problems, rather than find reasons to back out. Thirty Dragons' Den deals are proof of that."—WBW

The Uno was presented at the 2007 Intel International Science and Engineering Fair. "People went crazy for it," Ben recalls. "There was something about the aesthetics of the UNO that captured the imagination." *Popular Science* magazine instantly named the Uno Invention of the Year.

Based on the success of his prototype, Ben was invited to be on Dragons' Den. Only eighteen at the time, Ben didn't even have a business plan when he made his pitch. Even so, the five Dragons loved Ben— and loved the concept even more. He asked $1.5 million for 20 percent of the company. He got $1.25 million for 20 percent, with all five Dragons committing $250,000 on air.

"After the cameras stopped rolling, I learned the difference between reality TV and real life," Ben says. That's because eight months later, after the economic meltdown, he was down to one investor—just me. He took my $250,000 and scrambled to find replacement investors and eventually raised more money than he had been offered on the show—and at higher valuations.

Ben delayed his entry into the Massachusetts Institute of Technology (MIT) and spent another eighteen months developing the Uno. After a board was in place, he enrolled at MIT full-time. The board hired a CEO to run the company, but Ben was growing increasingly uncomfortable with its direction. Last year, he reduced his course load and took over as CEO. He restructured the company, now with a healthy $4 million in capitalization, and merged Uno into a new company called BPG Werks, focused on creating a strong brand presence in the extreme/power sport market. The company offers multiple innovative products that mix technology and fun.

Because its control systems are very complex, Uno is still years away from production. In order to find a steady revenue stream, Ben made a strategic decision to put the UNO on the back burner and focus on building a strong brand presence in the quickly growing extreme/power sport market by offering a variety of vehicles that provide new opportunities for adventure lovers to go fast in strange and exciting places.

Boston-based BPG Werks's first commercial vehicle offering to the public is the DTV Shredder, a "gnarly" off-road vehicle that the rider stands on—a mix between a skateboard and a Segway. Outfitted with tank treads, skateboard trucks and a powerful 4-stroke engine, the DTV Shredder can travel up to thirty miles per hour on snow, sand, trails and even mountainsides. It's getting attention from extreme sport athletes, recreational riders and gadget enthusiasts looking for new thrills. Ben showcased an early version of this product in Season 4 of Dragons' Den.

Ben now has twelve full-time people on payroll, working on everything from design to promotion, but he still doesn't have a fully marketable version of the UNO. Ben admits that finding ongoing funding to support day-to-day operations has been his biggest challenge. "Fortunately, I seem to have a knack for raising money."

Ben says evolving the company from a single- to multi-product focus has been a challenge. Merging two companies, one producing the UNO, the other producing the Shredder, was a big decision. "The majority of investors had money in both companies," says Ben, "but some didn't. The valuation of the two companies was different. Getting UNO investors to be okay with the merger and dissolving the board was a big hurdle. There were lots of heated emails, but hands down, it was the right thing to do."

Ben says taking a back seat to the CEO was the toughest part of the last few years. "It was hard to stand by and watch while someone else made the decisions," he says. Now that he's taken over the role, Ben has assembled a group of advisors in the Boston area to help him avoid the errors many start-ups can make. Ben is now looking forward to building an iconic brand. "I like the idea of creating an empire—modelled after Bombardier—based on a strong power-sport brand that reaches into other sectors like the military." The DTV Shredder already has five thousand pre-orders.

Here is a man who dreams of great swaths circling wheat fields, who dreams of lucid and crystal lakes, who dreams the restless dance of movement. Here is a man who has the energy to wait.

Here is a man who will infuse confidence with blue light. Eyes forward, a face to meet the faces that converge, waiting them out. Calmness modified. An intricate enigma, staring at the sun, staring straight into the scrutiny of the screen shot. Direct and unflinching; this is what you get.

Waiting for the moment to arrive with its quandary or consequence, waiting for patience itself. He's in no hurry to hurry. Hands clasped, as if to warrant the pause, that gentle attentive prelude to the palms opening, the hands suggesting solution.

Pure anticipate. Expectation defied in the wait, the intermission, the quick lilt of delay and appraisal. He is incipient energy, coiled attention, a bachelor quest. He is the problem of representation, decided in the pose of the subject, musing, expectant, biding his time.

This man conveys nothing stationary about waiting. He is ambivalence and wariness, but hope too, and compassion.

Shoes at the ready, prepared for motion, toes forward, inceptive action. Wait for the moment.

—Aritha van Herk

Eight

Philanthropy Is Good Business

I happen to believe philanthropy is good business. I know from personal experience that charitable giving can be one of the best ways to grow a business. The best corporate philanthropy doesn't just make a social impact, it also adds to a company's bottom line.

Most companies give out of a sense of obligation. I have always given out of a sense of opportunity, with the goal of not only making my community better, but of making my company bigger as well. I know that some people object to the notion of getting something from giving. But businesses *should* expect a return on their charitable donations. Realistically, there's no such thing as pure altruism. Nor should there be. In my world, giving and getting go hand in hand. Businesses and non-profits can mutually benefit from collaborative relationships. The best way to do that, in my view, is to see philanthropy as a tool for corporate growth.

I believe that companies will become better—and bigger—donors when they start seeing community giving as an opportunity rather than any sort of obligation. For those who might disagree with me, think hard about this: charitable giving that in turn reaps an economic return creates stronger companies that can make more meaningful contributions to their communities in the long run.

The Three Core Life Courses

When I talk to students or academics or frankly any other audience about opportunities for doing good, I suggest to them there are three ways anyone can maximize his or her impact on and in the world: they can offer their time, their money and their leadership. To me, a direct line to doing good in all aspects of life involves three core competencies. These are the three key or core life courses—and I encourage everyone to study them, and keep studying them throughout their lives.

We as a society need to think more clearly about what each student needs to have at the end of the journey. Every student needs a bundle of knowledge, skills and experiences. The first group of students who graduate with my three subjects—marketing, entrepreneurship and philanthropy—as part of their core curriculum will be a dramatically different calibre of student. But until everyone speaks the same vernacular we're not going to change the quality of student we produce. Until it has become core curriculum, it's just another elective, and the impact will be negligible.

These core subjects will develop students' leadership skills. And if we're going to drive innovation and productivity, it's as important to *fill* the bus with leaders as it is to have leaders *driving* the bus. As University of Calgary President Elizabeth Cannon eloquently stated during our discussion on the subject, "We need to develop our students as whole people, being able to work across disciplines and across sectors. That's how we are going to make great citizens."

> *"Students of all ages should study and learn three core life subjects: marketing, entrepreneurship and philanthropy."—WBW*

I couldn't agree more. I can even see combining these three subjects into a single mandatory class called "Changing the World." After all, when you're doing good, whether through marketing, entrepreneurship or philanthropy, you are, in fact, changing the world.

1. Marketing

Whether you're a dentist or an employee in an oil and gas company, everyone needs to market themselves and their ideas. You might be pitching your boss or perhaps a group of potential investors. In either case, being able to make your case effectively is essential. I made my fortune as an engineer working in finance but it was my knowledge of—and passion for—marketing that made the difference. Maybe you can build the next great invention, but if you can't sell it, you don't have a business.

Students who leave schools without understanding marketing have a gap in learning, and we need to close that gap. Much of my philanthropic success has resulted from a marketing mindset. I often refer to myself as an entrepreneurial philanthropist because I apply marketing approaches to my charitable work. In a very significant way, marketing levers the impact of both business and philanthropic pursuits. That's why it's so valuable.

2. Entrepreneurship

Students at every stage are seeing that the real world has opportunity, and they're finding ways to connect their knowledge and passion with what the world needs. I have an ongoing beef with academia because it normally links entrepreneurial studies with small business. That's a mistake. Entrepreneurship is a way of thinking. Small business is simply how many entrepreneurs start. When Murray Edwards built the Horizon Oil Sands Project inside Canadian Natural Resources Limited, he was being very entrepreneurial, but there was nothing "small business" about that process.

Unfortunately, entrepreneurial studies are usually confined to business schools. But the entrepreneurial process is relevant every-where. A few years ago I made a multi-million-dollar commitment to fund the Wilson Centre for Entrepreneurial Excellence out of the University of Saskatchewan. The mandate of the school is to inspire innovation and entrepreneurial thinking in all colleges and disciplines at the university. Nursing and fine arts and engineering students, as well as those from every other college, are encouraged to find ways to connect their learning with entrepreneurial opportunities.

With a little inspiration, an art historian could—as an entrepreneur—become one of the next great gallery owners, but we need to plant that seed early. I'm proud to say the WCEE has become a significant innovation incubator, connecting students and business leaders with investment opportunities focused on western Canada. These new ventures are part of the economic engine of our region, and each one, in its own way, is contributing "good" back to the larger community.

3. Philanthropy

The first thing we need students to understand is that investing in community is not an expense, but an investment. Schools and universities can be part of the process of changing that perception. Let's ask students important questions such as: What's working? What's not working? What else can we do? What sort of effort can or should you put into philanthropy? What should you expect in return? By making philanthropy part of a core curriculum, we're able to extend the conversation to every student.

Doing Good Isn't Just about Charity

Most people associate doing good solely with charitable initiatives. But I would argue that we shouldn't be so quick to separate the good that is generated by a successful business from the good that is generated by effective philanthropy. In my mind, the two are undeniably linked. It's no secret that my own financial success in business has allowed me to fund my considerable philanthropic work. In the same way, the smartest and most successful businesses are finding ways to use philanthropy not only to create social good, but also to create an economic benefit for themselves. This win-win scenario allows strong businesses to grow even stronger, and give back exponentially more.

One of my life goals is to encourage a redefinition of what changing the world really means. In my career, I have participated in financing some three to four hundred start-ups. A few have failed brilliantly, while others have enjoyed incredible success. Those start-ups—and thousands like them around the country—are making a tremendous impact on the lives of the people who work for them and the communities in which they operate.

Philanthropy Can Build

Businesses have a vested interest in creating better communities. Strong communities are able to attract new businesses, corporate head offices and a more educated workforce, which in turn create an even stronger business climate. Employees want to live in communities with a robust economic *and* social fabric, places where they feel connected to each other and enjoy a great quality of life. Better than anyone else, non-profit organizations know how to build these "sticky" communities. According to business guru Peter Drucker, the management of the social sector will largely determine the values, vision, cohesion and performance of twenty-first-century society. That's a tremendous responsibility, and one that we in the business world can help achieve.

It's no accident that some of the most successful entrepreneurs are also some of the most powerful philanthropists. We have a knack for understanding problems, identifying creative solutions and effecting change. Countless community organizations have benefitted from the vision and passion of outstanding community leaders. Their legacy will live on

"Besides being one of the best ways to address the world's problems, charitable giving is also one of the best ways to grow a business."—WBW

through the many people they've influenced, not least of which is a new generation of philanthropists, including me.

The FirstEnergy Example

As one of the co-founders of FirstEnergy Capital Corp., I've seen the enormous impact one company can have. It would be nearly impossible to measure the number of lives that have been touched—and dramatically improved—by FirstEnergy's philanthropic work.

Beginning in 1993, FirstEnergy has provided, directly and indirectly, in excess of $10 million in donations to upwards of five hundred charities or community organizations. I have been moved to tears many times by some of the countless letters of appreciation from the various groups we've supported, and the positive stories we've helped make happen.

To be candid, FirstEnergy didn't set out to be a leader in corporate philanthropy. We did set out to be a leader in investment banking. And we used charitable giving as a marketing tool. Every time we gave a contribution to a charity, we were very open about the fact that we expected something in return. What we gained in the form of public recognition, co-branding with larger companies or recognition within the charity's network helped us to dramatically increase our profile, develop new partnerships and grow our client base.

> *"I think of myself as an entrepreneurial philanthropist, which means I use the entrepreneurial approaches that helped me succeed in business to enhance my philanthropic initiatives."—WBW*

This give-and-get approach paid enormous dividends for the firm. Nearly twenty years later, FirstEnergy is one of the energy industry's leading and most prolific investment banks. By whatever yardstick you use, we've succeeded in every possible measure. In the process, we've inspired others in our network to begin their own philanthropic initiatives. This spirit of giving is helping to make Calgary one of the greatest cities in the world.

Successful partnerships have to share a common vision, and our partnership at FirstEnergy Capital Corp. certainly did. Our vision was to create an investment bank with a conscience. In a very real sense, we built integrity into our business plan. Being professional, effective and profitable wasn't enough. We also wanted to be good. In fact, very good. We set out from inception to maintain the highest standards of integrity in all of our dealings. Not only did this commitment to ethics reflect our personal values, we also knew that it would be a powerful marketing differentiator.

As mentioned earlier, from day one, we decided to give 2.5 percent of pre-tax profits to charity. We decided on 2.5 percent partly because it was more than anyone expected and would help us stand out from the crowd. It was definitely more than other companies were giving. Around that time, fewer than one in thirty Canadian businesses claimed any charitable donations at all; on average the rest gave less than 1 percent of pre-tax profits. We wanted to do more.

FirstEnergy's commitment to community has been foundational to its success because we treated our charity budget as our marketing budget. Every time we made a contribution to a charity, we expected something reasonable in return, either in the way of public recognition, shared profile with another well-respected company or recognition within the charity's network of supporters.

Getting Noticed

When we first started making donations to charities I would make a point of sending the cheque (signed by myself and when possible another senior partner of the firm) directly to the CEO or executive director of the charity, with a copy going to the second-in-command. We would also send a copy of each cheque to selected board members, clients, potential clients and competitors (and their spouses) who were known supporters of that charity. Instead of lumping ourselves in with a list of donors captured on the back page of the charity's annual report, which would probably not get noticed, we made a point, at the cost of a letter or two, of building our brand with thousands of people who had the potential to help us with goodwill for FirstEnergy.

Use Leverage

The first significant corporate entertaining event that FirstEnergy undertook was in support of a local arts group that had approached our firm with a very novel event idea: a 1920s-themed evening in the newly acquired and renovated studios of the renowned Alberta Ballet. The party was pitched to us as a turnkey event: the arts group would be responsible for everything that was needed in terms of decor, food and beverages and entertainment. The request was for us to both cover the costs of the event *and* to make a meaningful donation to the charity. The challenge for our firm was that the total dollars involved were considerably greater than made sense for our firm—and yet most of my partners were onside with the concept and format of the event and were supporters of the cause. The challenge was in coming to grips with the cost.

We tossed around all sorts of ideas, short of asking our potential clients for donations (remember, we were a new firm with very few clients). Ultimately the thought arose—what about a partner for the event? While this was an obvious conclusion, we were unsure at first of how to find or select a partner whose clients mirrored ours, since we didn't want or expect a competitor to play along. We then considered the professional services that both we and our clients used, particularly accountants and lawyers. After much deliberation, because we did business with all major accounting firms and likely a dozen legal firms, we decided to reach out to the venerable and highly regarded firm Bennett Jones to partner with us for the benefit of Alberta Ballet.

To our delight, the pitch/suggestion was very well received and we were off to the races. The first order of business was the invitation list and the obvious problem that the lawyers wanted to invite some of our competitors (as their clients) and we wanted to invite other law firms (who directed business to us and worked with us). The list, however, was the only speed bump in the process of putting the event together.

The outcome of our collaboration was simply amazing, and we ended up running several joint corporate client–development events over the ensuing years with Bennett Jones. The leverage that both firms enjoyed by sharing an event for the benefit of charity (and of our clients, and therefore of our firms) was immeasurable. And it was during this sharing of brand that I coined the phrase *brand rub*, referring to the incredible benefit that our brand new firm enjoyed by rubbing its brand up beside that of what was arguably one of western Canada's premier law firms, with a lineage that extended back almost a century. We didn't realize when we approached BJs (as they were known) how valuable their brand would be to us. We simply wanted to leverage our then limited promotions budget, and hoped our offer to do event coordination would be welcomed by our partners. Over the years we went on to invite a number of key businesses in Calgary whose client bases overlapped ours as partners/sponsors/hosts of other client-development events.

The Manitoba Flood

The Manitoba flood in the spring of 1997 was the most severe flooding of the Red River since 1826. The people of Manitoba suffered well over $500 million in damages.

In response to a concern from some of our staff that there was no one taking local action to raise funds for the people of Manitoba, or for our friends and clients living there, FirstEnergy decided to try something new. We thought that by allocating all of our trading commissions on a given day to Manitoba flood relief we might be able to engage our client base to simply direct trades to us—without cost to them or their funds—and effectively donate to the cause. We got the word out to all our clients about our special trading day. At that time, a good trading day would have generated just over $100,000 in commissions. But on the day dedicated to Manitoba flood relief, we managed to raise well over four times that amount—the tally topped $450,000 when we reconciled late that night. Although we were an energy boutique, several clients saw to it that we were one of the top traders in Nortel and several mining and industrial stocks that day. Clearly the clients were looking for creative ways to direct funds to a cause that was gripping the nation. The day was an incredible team effort. It engaged the entire firm and all our clients, and in the process changed the internal and external perceptions of our firm.

We then set about leveraging our donation without descending into shameless self-promotion, but rather raising the profile of and celebrating what we and our clients had just accomplished. I had learned that the Calgary Flames and the *Calgary Herald* were doing a joint event at the Saddledome—basically a concert to raise funds for flood relief—only a couple of days after our initiative. We contacted both Ken King, who was the publisher of the *Calgary Herald* at that time, and Ron Bremner, who was then president of the Flames organization, to see if we could contribute what we had raised. I didn't know either of them, but I introduced myself, saying, "Hi, I'm a partner at FirstEnergy." (Yes, I did have to explain who we were!) "We just raised a little over $450,000 for Manitoba flood relief. We would be willing to roll our efforts into your event, and create a win-win, to inspire others to play along."

Ken and Ron (our new best friends) were in our offices early the next morning to work out the most effective way of including us. Long story short: instead of having one of the partners from FirstEnergy walk onto the stage to announce our contribution, we had Paige Knight, a leading member of our support team, carry our flag. I still remember being

> "I have never looked at charity as an obligation, but rather as an opportunity. An opportunity to change the world."—WBW

in a corporate box with Paige's family and a few others from our team when Paige went onstage near the end of the concert to make the "special announcement." There wasn't a dry eye in the arena when she read out the total that we, obviously with our clients' help, had raised for the cause. Together with our donation, the total amount raised that night was north of $500,000. Certainly the event took headlines for raising half a million dollars in one crack, but the press was very kind to our firm, not least because the partners refused to do any interviews, instead directing all queries to Paige. Clearly FirstEnergy was again showing corporate Calgary that it was here to stay—we weren't just testing the waters.

After that initial "trading day" event, we also raised significant funds for relief in the aftermath of the ice storm in Quebec in 1999, the devastating prairie drought in 2002 and the disaster that resulted in Slave Lake, Alberta, when forest fires encroached into the town in 2011. In total, FirstEnergy raised several million dollars for all four of these initiatives by creatively engaging clients and staff.

Charity Cheques—Admission to FirstEnergy Events

Calgary is a very festive town. Many businesses throw parties for their clients throughout the year. One of the ways FirstEnergy set itself apart in the community was to turn all of our parties, over time, into charitable fundraisers. These invitation-only parties were always free for staff, clients and friends of the firm, but there was still a price of admission: a charity cheque to be handed over at the door. No cheque, no entry.

The cheque-at-the-door concept evolved greatly over time. At one of our earliest events—a rodeo we hosted in 1995—we had some university drama students dressed up as gunslingers who would "hold up" guests with toy guns and a bucket, demanding contributions for charity. At our first event in the summer of 1995 we raised about $12,000 in cash at the gate. The next year, we got creative (or so we thought) and invited a group of women—okay, they were actually part-time Hooters servers—to do the same job the students had done the summer before. The whole idea flopped when we forgot to give instructions as we had the first year. As a result the women focused on handing out beer at the gate as servers would, and basically forgot to ask for donations. Our total charity take went down dramatically (but we still appreciated the beer-distribution services).

After the Hooters experience, we realized we needed to do things differently in order to be effective. It was then that we came up with the idea of having our guests provide a cheque payable to the charity of our choice, in an amount that we eventually, softly advised should be equal to "whatever you would spend on a fine dinner with a great bottle of wine," making the amount a personal decision. The cheques submitted range from less than $50 (although very few at that level, but it still happens, and we accept such cheques without comment or question) up quite often to the $1,000 to $5,000 range—and sometimes higher. People really do understand our events are purposed with raising funds, often for causes that are not mainstream or well known. We grew the initial $12,000 take back in 1995 to something greater than $250,000 per event some two decades later.

Over the years, FirstEnergy gained a reputation for throwing some of the most sought-after, hot-ticket events in the city, which was a key part of the reason they've been so successful as fundraisers. We have always made sure our events are unique, with the highest-quality entertainment, food and fun.

One of our best-known events, the rodeo I mentioned above, was originally billed as FirstRodeo, and very much a family event. Over the course of a decade it evolved to the very adult FirstRowdy, now a Stampede tradition for the oil patch. Held on the first Tuesday of the Calgary Stampede, this invitation-only party starts around 3 P.M. and runs until someone turns out the lights. We have featured well-known Canadian talent the likes of Colin James, Tom Cochrane, Emerson Drive, Doc Walker, Beverley Mahood and Randy Bachman to perform on our stages. Cowboy hats and torn blue jeans are everywhere, and the dance floor is always packed. This event helps the chosen charities gain profile with Calgary's oil patch elite, and engages the rest of the corporate community in supporting lesser-known local charities.

Employee Morale

One of the most compelling but overlooked benefits of corporate charity is its impact on employee morale. FirstEnergy's commitment to philanthropy has provided untold personal benefits to our staff, proof that it's truly impossible to give without getting back more in return.

Just as I have been, so too has FirstEnergy's staff also been personally touched by the countless letters of appreciation from the various community groups we've supported in our city. It was not unusual for staff members to come into the office on Monday and share appreciation for FirstEnergy's giving program after they themselves had run across someone on the weekend

"Money is great, but it really can't buy happiness. If you measure success by the size of your wallet, you're destined to be unhappy. The best measure of happiness is not the size of your wallet, but the size of your smile."—WBW

whose life had been touched by some aspect our corporate charitable work. We also actively encouraged our staff to become active participants in the philanthropic process. Our staff even developed a program where employees charged themselves $10 each to wear jeans on Fridays, with every penny going to charity. To add to the fun, we also did a raffle for the tax receipt associated with donating the cash collected. Just being smart. Over the years many members of our staff have told us that the firm's commitment to charity was part of how they found greater meaning in their own lives.

FirstEnergy Partner Initiatives

Being a business owner creates the opportunity to leverage the efforts and passions of your employee base, whether it is three people, three hundred people, or thirty thousand people, to become an army of philanthropists. At FirstEnergy, we were proud to have built a culture committed to giving back to the community, both through our corporate donations and events, and through our people.

Over the fifteen-plus years I was actively involved, FirstEnergy never once turned down a client request or an employee suggestion for placing charitable funds. We didn't always give the amount that was requested, but we were there 100 percent of the time with support at some level. We also encouraged staff to invest their own resources, both time and money, to support the causes they cared about, and we celebrated them for their efforts. I will share just a few of the adventures in philanthropy undertaken by my colleagues as examples of their active participation.

FirstEnergy co-founder and CEO Jim Davidson has served on the board of the Calgary Humane Society since 2006 and successfully co-chaired their successful capital campaign, Leaps and Bounds, which provided the Humane Society with a new, $10-million, state-of-the-art facility that will serve Calgary for decades to come. While animal welfare is close to everyone's heart, Jim found out first-hand how far the issue can be from everyone's wallets, making this a very difficult campaign that very few could have succeeded at.

For many years, managing director Martin Molyneaux, an avid road-biking enthusiast, has participated in the national Ride for Diabetes Research fundraiser. Martin has personally raised hundreds of thousands of dollars over the years, making him one of the leading fundraisers for this cause in Canada.

Trout Unlimited has a mission to conserve, protect and restore Canada's freshwater ecosystems and their cold-water resources for current and future generations. Now retired as managing director, Rafi Tahmazian has organized some of the most successful fundraising dinners in North America in support of Trout Unlimited, raising millions for this initiative.

Decidedly Jazz Danceworks is a registered charity founded in Calgary to re-ignite the traditional values of jazz dance. Dance education is a vital component of DJD's mission, which includes community outreach and innovative artistic performances. Also retired as managing director, Scott Inglis is often cited for his efforts a decade ago, both on the board and as a key fundraiser, as the reason this program is alive today.

Since 2005, retired managing director William Lacey has run Calgary's Harvest ½-Marathon and in the process also raised hundreds of thousands of dollars. Together with FirstEnergy, he has helped to put in place much of the future funding requirement for Jamie's Preschool, a program that provides play, learning and support for children facing cancer, blood disorders and other critical illnesses.

Another admirable initiative was undertaken by our director of institutional research, Cody Kwong, for Christmas 2005. Cody's sister-in-law asked him to fill in as Santa at the last minute, when the scheduled Santa for the Discovery House Women's Shelter had to cancel on the women and children seeking refuge in the shelter over the holidays. Cody's olive complexion left him unsure of his credibility as Santa, but he took on the task with passion. The next year he sought support from his office colleagues in what has become an annual appearance as Santa. His efforts have raised more than $130,000 for Discovery House—very much in keeping with the FirstEnergy way of doing things differently.

Follow Our Lead

FirstEnergy's commitment to community inspires passion in our employees, and a spirit of giving that permeates our organization.

If you truly believe in creating and encouraging a culture of giving, then celebrate your employees who embrace that spirit. I recommend including time for volunteerism as a benefit in your organization. Provide time off, match or top up personal donations with corporate dollars and encourage people to raise money for worthy causes. Begin by modelling the behaviour you want to see. Then, celebrate, recognize and even reward it when you see it in others. Don't be concerned about the cost to your business of having your employees participate in volunteerism during company time; consider it a marketing or public relations expense, and make sure their efforts are noted publicly. The benefits will accrue. As I often say, giving is simply good business.

> *"I've made no secret of the fact that in my world, giving and getting go together. In fact, I believe businesses should expect a return on their charitable donations."—WBW*

Beyond the dollars raised and the impact on our own bottom line, FirstEnergy's philanthropic efforts have helped to engage our large network of business colleagues to create a better community, which, when you think about it, is critical for business success. Strong communities are able to attract new business development, encourage the relocation of corporate head offices and develop a more educated workforce, which in turn only enhances the business environment. More than that, it makes people feel attached to one another as neighbours and friends, enhancing a region's or community's quality of life and everyone's level of personal and professional success.

The Wilson Centre for Entrepreneurial Excellence

As an entrepreneur to the core, I love to be part of inspiring young people to embrace the power of entrepreneurship through my vision of planting seeds of entrepreneurship knowing that, with watering and care, they will someday grow into something interesting.

Not long ago, the opportunity came for me to connect my love of entrepreneurship with my passion for philanthropy. I have made a total $2.5-million gift to the University of Saskatchewan to establish and operate the Wilson Centre for Entrepreneurial Excellence (WCEE). The centre was the brainchild of Grant Isaac, the then dean of the newly sponsored N. Murray Edwards School of Business at my alma mater, the University of Saskatchewan in Saskatoon.

When we were in the planning stages for the Wilson Centre, we purposely developed it as a multi-disciplinary program that would transcend being a resource for just the school of business, which is what most people associate with entrepreneurship. Under the guidance of founding director Sanjeev Singh, the Wilson Centre developed a vision for becoming one of the pre-eminent centres for real excellence in entrepreneurship in Canada. With an economic, environmental and social consciousness, the centre's mandate is to inspire entrepreneurship and innovation among all college disciplines, and to connect business leaders, researchers and potential financiers with investment opportunities focused on western Canada.

Today, entrepreneurship classes or minors in entrepreneurship are open to virtually every undergraduate student in all major colleges within the University of Saskatchewan, embracing disciplines ranging from the liberal arts to kinesiology, and from engineering to agriculture and bioscience. The minor program has grown not only in numbers—almost seven hundred students campus-wide are currently enrolled in entrepreneurship classes—but it has helped spread a culture of respect and interest in entrepreneurship within the university community. As a result, entrepreneurial programming is under development for graduate students in pharmacy, health sciences, computer sciences and engineering.

The Wilson Centre also creates opportunities for students and the business community to meet and share ideas. Student innovators have had many opportunities to network and build associations with business professionals through various programs. The North Saskatoon Business Association recently reached out to the WCEE to find five top young entrepreneurs to compete for their Most Promising Young Entrepreneur Award at their annual Business Builder event. The evening actively engaged the business community with these young entrepreneurs, who were thoroughly impressed by the quality of ideas and professionalism these young individuals brought to the table. With time I hope to be able to fund similar programs at other institutions across Canada as part of a continuing program to plant the seeds of entrepreneurship as widely as possible. I see this not only as a charitable initiative, but also as the best investment I might be able to make in our great nation.

Here is a man who collects fun, gathers it up and reaps its vintage. Wait for it, the flare, the burst of fireworks. The long nights, the quick connections, the fierce come-ons no snobbery but the canopy of fun.

Theories of fun, faces of fun, the rocketing speed of fun, the slowness of fun, the fun of fun. Get ready, shoes laced, no logic to this, but happiness and its outcome, time shortened to an instant, and the costumes can wait, the fun is about to begin.

Here's the primary category of action: make every moment rollick, no logic but logic, no activity but pleasure. The difference between enjoyment and fun is that one is diversion and one is pure pleasure and anticipation, spontaneous, without reserve, no time like the present, no present like delight and delectation, systemic fun, let the fun begin. Outcome: happiness quotient, the greatest return. Laughter and forgiveness, speculation and other etymologies of delight.

Ready for takeoff. To make merry, and to make of merry an outcome, filled with gladness. Ah, the delight.

Here is a man for whom fun is more than diverting, but the delight of high spirits, the infinite reach of pleasure in every moment of thought. Relish, savour, gusto, and let predictability be damned.

—Aritha van Herk

Nine

Creative Philanthropy

What I didn't expect when I started out on this journey is how much my philanthropic work would impact me personally. As many of you already know, financial success can be surprisingly hollow. So after spending many years focused on making money, I now spend as much, if not more, of my energy giving it away. One of my greatest rewards has come from connecting people to their own potential for doing good. As more people see how easy it is to make a big difference in the lives of others, they engage their friends in the experience, and the circle of influence grows, multiplying the impact of all.

A Very Personal Return on Investment

I know a lot of people who are on the fence when it comes to personal giving: some are big donors, others are not so engaged. For those of you who haven't bought into the value of personal giving, I have one question for you. What else are you planning to do with your money? There are only so many toys you can buy before you realize that there's more to life than playthings. I realized a while ago that the big bank account, nice house, vacation home, cars, boats and vacations still left me with the vague feeling that I had the capacity for something more—and *more* didn't mean more deals. One of the best ways

I know to find real and lasting significance in life is to enrich the lives of others. I know how clichéd that sounds, but it's true.

Here's another truth: If you think you're going to do your children a favour by leaving them a big inheritance, think again. Intergenerational wealth transfer is one of the most serious issues of our time. I've seen some families appear to do this well, but I've seen others who cripple their children with kindness. My own kids know that the bulk of my wealth will go to charity. I won't leave them destitute, but I also won't hamstring them with more than they appear to need. None of my children will live expecting an inheritance because, frankly, there won't be one from me. To my delight, each of my now-adult children is finding a career path based on their respective personal passions, which I applaud.

I recognize that this is an extremely personal decision. But I encourage you to consider what really is best for your children. I agree with American billionaire and philanthropist Warren Buffett, who said, "I want to give my kids just enough so that they would feel that they could do anything, but not so much that they would feel like doing nothing." When you're considering your own estate transfer, the appropriate or suitable threshold for giving to the next generation is probably lower than you might first think.

The bottom line is this: When you "get hit by the bus" and your life comes to an end, you've got two places to send your money: children or charity. I'm not a big fan of waiting for the reading of the will to find out where one's parents' money is going. For me, the bigger and better plan is to give where the money will do the most good, and the best way to manage the process is while I'm alive.

Many approaches to philanthropy can be dull and uninspiring. If you've done the fundraising dinner circuit as much as I have, you know what I'm talking about—silent auctions, rubber-chicken dinners and speeches that put you to sleep.

I think of myself as an entrepreneurial philanthropist, which means I use the entrepreneurial approaches that helped me succeed in business to enhance my philanthropic initiatives. I believe strongly that creativity, a strong marketing focus and strategic partnerships can and should be used to engage more people to support non-profit work. Events and campaigns need to be *memorable* to raise awareness and funds.

I think too few people are truly creative in using corporate fund-raising events to give a full-blown sensory experience to their guests. Events have the power to drive home the significance of a cause, engaging people emotionally as well as intellectually, and turning them into committed donors rather than just passive participants. All it takes is a little imagination.

A great deal of my time has been spent on personal initiatives in support of a variety of charities, helping to raise awareness and funds for one cause after another, serially, and then moving on to the next cause. I try to take an entrepreneurial approach to each event, making sure that each one remains front and centre with the potential donors for its future benefit. I will share an overview of some of the wide range of initiatives I have already been involved with. Just know that the wheels are spinning as I look for new opportunities.

> *"Don't forget to give something back. No act of charity is too small. Focus on making money—but also focus on making a difference in your community."—WBW*

My First Fundraising Initiative: Kilimanjaro

Shortly after finishing my cancer treatment in 2001, I decided to test my strength by climbing Mount Kilimanjaro, the highest peak in Africa, with a team of climbers raising funds for the Alzheimer Society of Canada. Keith Harradence, a friend from my days at the University of Saskatchewan, and his wife, Susan Ormiston of CBC fame, were two of the key organizers of this trip as a tribute to Susan's late mother who had succumbed to the disease.

Every climber committed to raise at least $10,000 and to pay their own expenses. My initial plan was to simply make the donation of

$10,000 and not ask anyone else to participate in my adventure, which I regarded as a very personal journey. The notion of directly asking for funds was new to me. A neighbour offered to send "ask letters" to a list of downtown business types for me and I declined. When he pressed me for the third time (Thank you, Gordon Dixon!) I capitulated and decided to do my own letter—just five days before departing for Africa. My assistant, Christina, and I used a FirstEnergy-based marketing list we used for inviting people to events, and then wrote and rewrote a dozen times my own ask letter. We printed off slightly more than a thousand letters and I then personally signed and added a note to *every* single letter, while Christina labelled and stuffed the envelopes. From the start of the project to the point when every letter was either with the courier or in the mail, only thirty-six hours elapsed. I was signing letters from suppertime until 4 A.M. the next morning, but as my dad often said, "A job worth doing is worth doing right." I didn't have the luxury of time, but I wanted my first ask to be done right. (As an aside: to this day, I still toss any and every donation-request letter that comes to me machine-signed or signed by an assistant for the big boss.)

How did it go? This is what my fellow climber Keith Harradence remembers:

> To participate, each climber was pressured or compelled to raise $10,000 for the cause. When we started the climb, we knew that Brett hadn't had a chance to do any real fundraising. But when we got about two-thirds up the mountain, we got news that the thousand or so letters that he had personally signed just before jumping on the airplane for the trip had raised over $300,000. That's just the way he is. Brett in a week could raise $300,000.

The exercises—both the climb and the letters—were a success by every possible measure: the right ask, the right cause and the right time.

My Second Fundraising Initiative: Head-Shave

The Kids Cancer Care Foundation of Alberta (KCCFA) is a charitable organization that helps build bridges of hope and pillars of support for families fighting childhood cancer.

In the summer of 2002 I was asked to join a group of seven businessmen in Calgary in a group head-shave. We were each asked to raise at least $10,000 towards a team goal of $100,000. As I had done when I climbed Kilimanjaro for the Alzheimer Society a year earlier, I again sent out a carefully worded letter requesting support to well over one thousand contacts in Calgary (and a selected few across Canada), and the response was simply overwhelming. In a few short weeks we raised over $375,000. The future of my hair was sealed.

> "The true meaning of life is to plant trees under whose shade you do not expect to sit."—Nelson Henderson

Now, to have a little fun along the way, I decided to dye my hair blond the day prior to the shave, since it was going anyway. The dye job was done at home by our children's nanny and I think it came out looking more like leopard spots than true blond. Nonetheless, it was a ton of fun. We stopped partway through the shave to see what I looked like with a Mohawk haircut. For a few minutes I flirted with possibly being the only investment banker in Canada to show up in the office with a Mohawk. There are pictures—but we don't post them!

The Battlefords: My Hometown

I've always had a big emotional connection to my hometown of North Battleford, Saskatchewan (and its sister town across the river, Battleford). But as I started becoming more focused on philanthropy, and raising the bar for my giving in Calgary, I realized I had done nothing substantial to give back to my home province. In 2003 I decided to change that.

I hired a friend from my university days, Sandy Vigrass, to help me look homewards. We contacted the local United Way and the regional Chamber of Commerce and asked them to provide us with the names of recommended local charities. From their list of seventy-five or so names, we focused on about sixty charities, based on the issues and initiatives that mattered most to me. We then sent a letter to each asking what they would do if a donor gave them between $1,000 and $3,000. In one page, I wanted to know how the money would be used, and what they would do to recognize the gift. Posing these questions forced each organization to think about *both* their ask and their offer.

We eventually landed on funding thirty charities through a $100,000 donation to the Battlefords' United Way. While I had done my homework on where I was directing my funds, it turned out I had not done much research on the lay of the charitable land in my hometown. I was surprised to learn that my single donation matched its entire annual fundraising goal. And until then, the biggest single donation the United Way had ever received was $5,000. I had always known that a lot of people in the Battlefords were wealthy. But it became apparent that they had never been given a vision for building their city through creative philanthropy. I believed there was a fair amount of money sitting under some mattresses in the two communities. It was time to shake some of it loose.

"Rather than guiding from the grave, I encourage people to experience the joy of giving while living."—WBW

On July 11, 1987, my grandmother passed away—she was in her late eighties—in the Battlefords Union Hospital (BUH). Then, less than an hour later, in the very same hospital, my mother also died, ending her brief battle with lung cancer at the young age of fifty-seven. Without dwelling on the incredible emotional impact of that evening and of the following days, with back-to-back funerals—I do like to think that my grandmother organized her time with us on earth to leave just before Mom, to lead the way and travel with her.

My family and I never forgot the compassion and professionalism that the staff of BUH showed us that difficult day, and in lockstep with my donations to the United Way, we decided to make a large donation to the hospital in memory of my mother and grandmother. I gave the BUH a call and asked, "What do you need these days?" They told me that they were desperate for a new X-ray machine. We made a $160,000 donation to make that happen. That donation, in conjunction with the $100,000 to the United Way, created headlines (without any press communication of any kind) and truly began to set the giving bar higher in the Battlefords.

The next year I phoned again and asked the CEO of the hospital, "What do you need this year?" This time he was more ambitious. He asked, "How much do you have to give?" I replied, "I'm not sure. Come back to me with your ask." I heard later that my request cost the CEO some sleep that week. He was genuinely concerned about asking too much. And yet he certainly didn't want to under-ask. He needn't have worried, because his response was brilliant.

His letter itemized a grocery list of needs with corresponding dollar amounts. "If you give us $5,000, this is how we'll spend the money. If you give us $10,000, this is how we'll spend it." He provided options for $20,000, $50,000, $100,000, $500,000 and million-dollar gifts, with an explanation of how each donation would be spent. I was impressed that he showed the same attention to detail at the $5,000 level as for $1-million level.

The request for four new anesthesiology machines caught my eye. The hospital had four operating rooms with four old units on-site. Because of the age of the units, they could only use two or three at a time, since at least one unit was down for repairs at any one time.

At $600,000, I knew I could make a major contribution towards the anesthesiology equipment, but I wanted to do more than just write a cheque. I told the hospital that I would give $300,000 towards the new machines, but they had to match my donation by raising

$300,000 themselves. I didn't know it, but until then, the most the hospital had raised during one campaign was $100,000. Once again—I hadn't asked the question—so I didn't pause to wonder if my offer was reasonable.

The hospital conditionally accepted my plan, but wanted twelve months to raise the money. I thought for a few minutes and gave them three months. I can only imagine the nervous conversations that took place at BUH that day, but they called back the next morning and agreed to the three-month challenge, and the Dollar-for-Dollar campaign was on. It ultimately took less than three months for the Battlefords to meet—and exceed—the BUH's fundraising goal.

They announced their fundraising victory on the local radio station at the end of a very touching and involving radiothon. They called me with the results: "Brett, we have met your challenge. In fact we blew through it, and have raised $500,000." I was so moved by the way the community had come together that there was little I could do now but match them dollar for dollar and up my donation to $500,000. The hospital was now sitting on $1 million. To say that they had surprised themselves would be an understatement.

Sometimes, the best way to encourage someone is by challenging them to do more than they think they can do. I am proud of this initiative because of the impact it had on the community in terms of dollars raised, for sure, but more especially in terms of the community engagement it inspired. If someone from four hundred miles away, who had moved away twenty years earlier, could believe in the Battlefords, then so could its citizens.

The Fiftieth Birthday Bash

This event became the perfect convergence of music, entertainment, marketing, promotion, connections, creativity and fun. Most importantly, it also represented my commitment to community.

I was on a father-son fishing trip off the coast of Vancouver Island in the summer of 2006, when I discovered that a number of friends, all community leaders and business leaders in their own right, were about to turn fifty by virtue of being born in 1957. As we kicked around ideas over breakfast about what each of us might be doing to celebrate the occasion, the concept of a meaningful charity event that could involve all of the "1957 Birthday Boys" began to percolate in my mind.

A few hours later, I was out on the ocean fishing with Keith MacPhail and our sons. During wide-ranging conversation about changing the world, I asked him if he would like to split the costs of a significant birthday party with me, backing a large fundraiser using our birthday celebrations as the launching point. He confided to me that his wife would be relieved if she didn't have to plan a big party, and admitted that what I had in mind sounded like a lot of fun. I had the first partner and had raised the first significant donation ('Thank you, Keith!). The game was on.

I started circulating the idea to more and more 1957 friends, most of whom toiled in the oil patch or in Calgary real estate and, amazingly, stumbled across almost twenty who were eligible to join the party. The more we talked, the more we got excited about what we could do as a group to celebrate a milestone and do something of enduring value for the community at the same time.

Eventually, thirteen Birthday Boys signed up with personal commitments totalling close to $1 million, and began to plan the largest semi-public birthday party Calgary had likely ever seen. We came up with the idea of booking some of the biggest entertainers from our era, and invited our friends and colleagues to enjoy the spectacular event—with a twist. Anyone attending the event was expected (not just asked) to bring a "meaningful" cheque for charity. And all donations would support the charity of our choice.

Early on, as a group, we considered supporting four or five charities that would enable us to make a broader impact. Only a few months before the party, we were still trying to short-list charitable causes when it struck me that there was no need to wrestle with the idea of multiple charities, when the one cause—as men—that we could all get behind was prostate cancer. I had already waged my personal battle with the disease, and more than a few of the Birthday Boys had been personally affected by it in some way. It was a common connection, and a cause that was worthy of our support. We realized ours was the perfect group to promote awareness and early detection among our peers and the larger community.

We agreed that the majority of the donations raised that night would be directed towards education and awareness of prostate cancer, encouraging men to get tested (the earlier the better—don't wait until you're fifty!) and to have annual and thorough physical exams. Most of the balance would be directed towards support and treatment, and improving access and more comprehensive care for men and their families. And any residual unallocated donations would be directed towards selected research projects that would address the core concerns of the group—prevention, diagnosis and treatment. To achieve these goals, we collaborated with Calgary's Prostate Cancer Institute, Prostaid Calgary and the Prostate Cancer Research Foundation of Canada.

Basically the Birthday Boys committed to funding the entire cost of the event with their sponsorship dollars so that all of the money collected from invited guests would go directly to the charity. Ultimately, each of us made a contribution to the cause in amounts ranging from $50,000 to $100,000 in order to bring the event to life. In return, each participant was able to invite from one hundred to two hundred people to the event.

> *"I also think of myself as a philanthropic entrepreneur—which means using charitable initiatives to help build a business—and getting value out of changing lives."—WBW*

Once the recipient of our fundraiser had been selected, we began to put the entertainment plan together. We chose Calgary's Jubilee Auditorium as the venue, and had the entire lobby decorated in a 1957 theme to celebrate the year of our birth. The menu included classic fifties food, including mini-burgers, celery and peanut butter or celery and Cheez Whiz, meatloaf and mac 'n' cheese. Guests were invited to dress in their favourite clothing from any of the different decades we have lived through—ideally the sixties or seventies. And we had fun with some extraordinarily creative marketing materials that included an online private micro-website that helped guests come up with costume ideas and created a lot of early buzz for the event.

On the night of the party, May 12, 2007 (chosen to suit all of the participants, to fall after the return of our children from university and before any high school graduation events), actors roamed the lobby playing our soon-to-be parents back in 1957. The women acting as our mothers appeared to be outrageously pregnant, and the fathers were suitably nervous. The whole show started when the pretend mothers had their water break. They then ran into the auditorium with the crowd in tow to see what was going to happen next. We launched the formal celebration by taking people back on a sentimental journey through the decades of our collective lives.

One of Canada's top comedians, Jebb Fink (okay: he is a transplanted American, but he so loves Canada), took us through the early years of our lives with a comedic bent. He worked in costume as a doctor celebrating our birth year, and then guided the audience through our growing-up years. He became a teacher trying to educate us, and then, for his finale, stumbled forward as a more-than-slightly-stoned hippy—apparently influencing this group of now roughly fifteen-year-old, and very impressionable, young men. There were tears of laughter from some of the parents in attendance who had lived through the era and understood the relevance of the jokes.

The Birthday Boys appeared in costume a few times. The first time, they rode onto the stage spread over a '57 Thunderbird convertible, James Dean fashion, in white runners, tight blue jeans and very tight white shirts (the boys had all worked out a *lot* prior to the event) to meet Beverley Mahood for her rendition of "Happy Birthday." Later the boys came out again in matching red-collared shirts over the same fitted jeans and white runners, this time to sing along to the classic song "American Pie," and to share in imbibing a toast to our birthdays with a bottle of 1957 single malt Scotch that we had scoured the liquor stores of the nation for. Fun? Yes—and then some.

Randy Bachman and Burton Cummings were meant to be the key performers as headliners of the evening, representing the music of The Guess Who and Bachman–Turner Overdrive, and they truly were. But while Bachman and Cummings were the undisputed stars, the other acts held their own. Peter Noone, from the iconic musical group Herman's Hermits, which lived in the shadow of only The Beatles, absolutely stunned the audience as our opening act. Every song in his hour-long set caused an audible gasp as everyone realized that *he* was the artist behind such classic songs as, "I'm Henry the VIII, I Am"; "Mrs. Brown, You've Got a Lovely Daughter"; "There's a Kind of Hush"; and "Bus Stop."

As mentioned, the event was structured to be invitation-only and sort-of free. "Free with a charity cheque." Rumour on the street before the event was that we were looking for donations of a thousand dollars per guest. That was simply not true. What we wanted were *meaningful* donations, which for some might mean the cost of a nice meal out, and for others, a lot more. At the event we showed a video about prostate cancer and what we wanted to do with the funds that were raised. Our moderator/host for the evening was a celebrated local TV talk-show celebrity, David Kelly, and he interviewed me about the history of our event and our underlying expectations. In the course of the interview, I shared a few key perspectives. First, on the importance of raising awareness of testing for prostate cancer at an early age, I said that too often "men just scratch issues below the belt until they go away." Humorous, yes; close to the truth—also yes! I then addressed what we meant by a meaningful donation and I made it clear that there was neither a minimum nor a maximum amount. We wanted everyone to give whatever they thought they could afford to give, making it meaningful to them. I often joke that to make a donation meaningful to me, you should either add another dollar or double the amount, depending on the audience. My point is never to appear ungrateful for the contribution given but to remind everyone that we can always do a little more.

After that little pep talk, dozens of guests doubled their original donation, so in the end we raised more than $100,000 over the amount that was originally committed. One of the Birthday Boys even contributed an extra $50,000 above his original and agreed donation. But it was one of my daughter's best friends, Sara, barely out of high school, who walked up to me at the end of the night with a twenty-dollar bill, wanting to double her opening donation. Of all the donations we received that night, for me, that one was the most touching. I still am easily moved by her action.

In addition to asking for meaningful donations, we decided to invite by private letter a small number of people to effectively become sponsors of the event. We pre-established a series of donor recognition levels and sent personalized requests to about two hundred people roughly six weeks beforehand. With an incredible response rate of almost 50 percent, we raised almost $2.4 million in pledges (including the contributions of the Birthday Boys). In combination with almost $700,000 in cheques brought to us at the door, we finished the night with just over $3 million for the fight against prostate cancer, an astonishing and possibly record-breaking amount of money for a single-night fundraiser in this neck of the woods at that time.

Subsequently I was told that the event, which we proudly called Taking Care of Business (Thank you, Tom Cross!), was one of the most successful one-night fundraisers the country had ever seen. It was a one-shot deal, not put on by a team of hundreds of volunteers and planners, but rather, by a handful of people: myself; my assistant, Christina; our event planner extraordinaire, Jocelyn Flanagan; the senior creative team at Zero Gravity; and, of course, the Birthday Boys and their incredible networks. But in addition to raising money, we also did something even more impressive: according to some in the cancer world, we did more to raise awareness about prostate cancer prevention in one night than had been achieved in the previous decade. The impact of the event became more apparent a few days later, when well-known national columnist Don Martin's story on the event, and the philanthropic leadership involved, ran as a page-three feature in most of the major newspapers across Canada—not faint praise for a birthday party, eh?

Ultimately all our goals for the evening were accomplished. The birthdays were celebrated. Guests were entertained. Funds were raised. And, most importantly, awareness of prostate cancer was really lifted, and all with a glowing spirit of entrepreneurial philanthropy.

The Garden Party

Loosely based on a shared birthday celebration that my July first birthday twin, Heather Shaw, and I put together back in 2004, this event has evolved away from the somewhat traditional birthday celebration for a few hundred friends with a charity angle, into a focused celebration for various charitable causes with an invitation list approaching fifteen hundred family, friends, staff, partners, clients and "influencers" of all sorts. Confirmed attendees approach one thousand. I now host the Garden Party towards the end of June each year in the relatively large yard behind and beside my home. I use it as a chance to bring together people from my various networks to officially kick off summer, with great food and unusual wine, and always with unique entertainment. Performing guests have included the incomparable The Canadian Tenors; the one and only Sarah McLachlan; my very talented music partners, Beverley Mahood and Carol Welsman; as well as the child piano virtuoso Christian Laurian. We have recently brought in the up-and-coming country act Brett Kissel; internationally renowned violinist Sophie Serafino; the recent Juno Award winner for Best New Artist in Canada, Meaghan Smith; and one of the world's greatest spoken-word artists, from the stage of the Vancouver 2010 Winter Olympic Games opening ceremonies, Shane Koyczan.

The Garden Party is always a great excuse to celebrate, but we never miss the opportunity to do something good for a cause. The event now generates from $200,000 to $400,000 each year, usually in support of causes that are outside the limelight, where the benefit of the increased attention is often as valuable as the funds raised. The format of the Garden Party (like all of the FirstEnergy events I have quarterbacked) has me paying 100 percent of the costs of the event, and expecting all attendees (and hopefully many of those invited but unable to attend) to either bring or send cheques payable to the featured charities. That allows one hundred cents out of every dollar I raise to flow through to the chosen charities.

As I appeal to the philanthropist in each of you, remember that parties or events don't ever have to be as elaborate as mine. Consider hosting a dinner for a cause you care about and, in addition to their favourite dish, ask your guests to bring along a cheque for charity.

> *"Anything you do out of a sense of obligation is going to have a different outcome than when you act out of a sense of opportunity."*—WBW

You'll be amazed at how one small act or suggestion can cause a chain reaction of good in your inner circle. Here is more information on the causes that have been close enough to my family and me to merit presenting as the lead charities for the last six Garden Parties:

2007: Right to Play

Right to Play is an athlete-based international humanitarian organization that uses sport and play to aid the development of children and youth in underprivileged areas of the world.

After her gold medal performance in Torino in 2006, speed skater Clara Hughes made an emotional and inspiring $10,000 donation to Right to Play. She challenged all Canadians to follow her lead, and so I did, immediately making my own donation of $10,000—in fact, I emailed her my commitment at 4 A.M., as I was up to watch her skate the 5,000-metre final. After that, I took the time to get to know Clara personally and learned more about the incredible work this organization is doing around the world.

Because I have seen the power of sport in my own children's lives, I wanted my family, friends and business colleagues to learn about Right to Play and the difference their programs are making in children's lives and communities across Africa, Asia and the Middle East by featuring the organization as the recipient charity of my 2007 Garden Party.

Since Clara was unable to attend that year, other Right to Play ambassadors, Hayley Wickenheiser, Kristina Groves, Arne Dankers and Canadian National Director Warren Spires willingly filled in. Hayley, Kristina and Arne spoke to my guests and presented me with a Right to Play hockey jersey with "Wilson" emblazoned on the back as a memorable birthday present.

Proceeds from the Garden Party were directed towards the Rwanda Challenge, in which child development programs give to Rwanda's children, many of whom lost their parents during the hundred-day genocide in 1994. Others are orphaned because of the AIDS virus, and are among the growing number of children who carry the virus. Right to Play uses play as a teaching tool to help children understand how the virus can spread to others, part of Right to Play's Live Safe, Play Safe program, which focuses on disease prevention.

2008: Little Warriors

Glori Meldrum, a survivor of childhood sexual abuse, is a friend whom I met through YPO. She decided to turn her very negative childhood assault and related experiences into something positive by creating a national organization focused on education about and prevention of child sexual abuse.

Little Warriors teaches adults how to help prevent, recognize and react responsibly to child sexual abuse. In addition to prevention education, Little Warriors also provides information about the prevalence and frequency of child sexual abuse and information about healing and support resources. When she decided to launch her organization, I was happy to help introduce her to the Calgary community in 2008. Here's what Glori says about the impact of the party:

> Brett was one of the first people to stand up and help us financially. The Garden Party raised just over $100,000 and gave us room to breathe as a start-up organization. Because Brett stood up with his time, money and endorsement, others followed his lead and supported Little Warriors.

Glori runs her own advertising agency in Edmonton. She has used her skill as a marketer and her relationships with media outlets to generate millions of dollars in donated advertising to help raise awareness for the issues and her cause.

2009: 777 Run for Sight

Most people are winded after twenty-four minutes of running, let alone twenty-four miles. Norma Bastidas is an ultra-marathon runner. She sometimes races for twenty-four hours straight, takes a forty-five-minute nap, and then does it again. She competes in the most gruelling races on earth, having crossed the blistering deserts of the Sahara, endured the sub-zero temperatures of the Antarctic and navigated the thick jungles of Brazil. During one race alone, Norma ran up and down the total height of Mount Everest, climbing and descending more than 10,000 metres above sea level in one race.

With the help of truly world-famous and world-class ultra-marathon runner Ray Zahab, on July 11, 2009, Norma became the first person in history to run seven true ultra-marathons on all seven continents in seven consecutive months, covering more than 1,400 kilometres, or an average distance in each race of some two hundred kilometres.

The motivation for the race came from her eldest son, Karl. Several years earlier, at the age of eleven, Karl was diagnosed with a degenerative condition, one-rod dystrophy. There is no cure for this condition, and it can result in significant vision loss, even blindness. As a single mother supporting herself and her two sons, Norma was emotionally drained following Karl's diagnosis. To relieve the stress, she started running. In 2007, with only a half marathon and a full marathon under her belt, she registered to run her first ultra in support of the Canadian National Institute for the Blind (CNIB). The race was a gruelling 125-kilometre trek that included a more than 5,000-metre elevation change over three mountain summits. After suffering from hypothermia near one of the mountaintops, Norma didn't complete her first ultra race. But the question was planted in her mind: If she could go ninety-four kilometres without any real training, how far was she capable of going with training?

Norma was inspired to organize a run that literally covered the globe to raise awareness for a disease that is reaching epidemic proportions, affecting more than 160 million people, mostly in developing countries.

Norma saw the ultra-marathon experience as a metaphor for the trials faced every day by the visually impaired. While ultras are tough physically and mentally, the challenge to the runner is only temporary. But people with visual impairments overcome enormous challenges every day of their lives in a battle that never ends, according to Norma.

Through her determination and commitment, Norma showed her son Karl that he is not alone in his fight. Her around-the-world run generated local, national and international media attention, and generated almost $200,000 in donations for the three organizations behind her efforts: the CNIB, the Foundation Fighting Blindness and Operation Eyesight. She was so inspiring to me that I made her 777 Run for Sight the recipient charity of the 2009 Garden Party.

Norma is a powerful example of the challenge commonly attributed to Gandhi to "be the change you wish to see" in the world.

2010: Boomer's Legacy

Boomer's Legacy is focused on helping women and children in Afghanistan and, by extension, honouring our soldiers who have served there, especially those who have made the ultimate sacrifice.

Boomer's Legacy is named for Corporal Andrew James Eykelenboom, a Canadian medic who was killed by a suicide bomber in Spin Boldak, Afghanistan, in August 2006 when he was twenty-three. While serving in Afghanistan, Andrew (known to his friends as "Boomer") recognized numerous opportunities for assisting the Afghan people through the distribution of medical supplies, educational material, books and warm clothing. In small, personal ways, Boomer and his comrades felt they were able to make a special contribution to bringing peace and stability to Afghanistan. Boomer's Legacy has been created to further these accomplishments.

During my 2010 Garden Party, we raised $250,000 for Boomer's Legacy. Honoured guests included business and community leaders, politicians (including The Honourable Peter MacKay, Minister of National Defence) and representatives from my various Dragons' Den projects.

2011: Dare to Care

I was introduced to Dare to Care through Kim Edwards, the wife of one of my business colleagues. The issue certainly resonated, and I was impressed by the brilliant simplicity of this program. Volunteers engage students in opportunities to share their experiences with bullying, whether as a victim, perpetrator or bystander, and so encourage them to empathize with one another, and to forgive and hold one another accountable. The Dare to Care program involves students, teachers, parents and the community in an effort to eliminate bullying and other dangerous behaviours from schools and to create an atmosphere of tolerance and respect.

Shortly before my 2011 Garden Party, I learned that the twelve-year relationship between Dare to Care and its corporate sponsor had recently ended. After a conversation with the co-founder of the program Lisa Dixon-Wells, I decided to make Dare to Care my charity of choice. The event was, on every level, a major success. But the real success was the $325,000 raised to help teach children to stand up to bullying.

2012: Eating Disorders

In 2012, we chose three causes, all focused at least in part on eating disorders, an issue that hits close to home for many of us—including my extended family. Eating disorders are the number one chronic illness facing today's youth. They have the highest mortality rate of any mental illness and are having an enormous impact on our world. Yet awareness of their prevalence and understanding of what they are is low.

Three organizations—BodyWhys Youth Canada, Juno House and the Calgary Counselling Centre—were beneficiaries of the proceeds of the event. BodyWhys is the only registered charity in Canada solely focused on preventing eating disorders. BodyWhys provides social support, physical resources and mental resiliency to help youth grow up happy and healthy, free from disordered eating and self-harming behaviours. BodyWhys helps open the door to the largely unknown world of eating disorders, providing critical inside knowledge in a useable, actionable way to deliver answers, clarity and hope.

Juno House specializes in the unique problems and challenges that girls, young women and their families encounter in our increasingly difficult world, building their capacity for emotional health, while inviting their parents to develop a more coherent understanding of themselves and their children. Juno House provides counselling and related services to address issues related to eating disorders—self-esteem, trauma, anxiety, depression and self-harm. Their goal is to help girls learn to speak in exclamations!!!!

The Calgary Counselling Centre's (CCC's) eating disorder program works with women, men, boys and girls between the ages of twelve and sixty who struggle with an eating disorder. The centre provides individual, couple, family and group therapy, as well as nutritional counselling and medical consultation. The CCC's programs are receiving national and international attention for their ability to successfully meet client needs and profoundly impact people's lives.

This year's Garden Party raised more than $350,000 for eating disorders, but as those attending will attest, we did more good by raising awareness of the issue than money can buy.

The Christmas Charity Concert

Back in the fall of 2006, Beverley Mahood and I compared notes on the idea of staging a Christmas Concert for families and friends—with a charity angle, of course—in which we would inject a small-town feel with a potluck reception prior to the event. We found a church and launched another event, this time in support of the Calgary Veterans Food Bank, a program that supplies veterans in the area with so much more than food. Support for the veterans ranges from prosthetics and clothing to cash to help with rent or mortgage payments.

I now run the Christmas Charity Concert every year, usually in a local church in the week before Christmas. Beverley has participated when her schedule has permitted. We have enjoyed artistic support from David Kelly and Jebb Fink as MCs, Kalan Porter (the first Canadian Idol winner), The Canadian Tenors, and Carol Welsman. The folk duo the Compadres—James Keelaghan and Oscar Lopez—have unearthed their treasure of Christmas songs for this event, as have Christian Laurian, Brett Kissel, Sophie Serafino and MacKenzie Porter (a.k.a. The Black Boots). Not to be forgotten, Sara Staples—a young Calgarian with a master's degree in operatic arts from the University of California, Los Angeles—has graced our stages almost every year. From Dragons' Den, we have found comic support from Clark Robertson, the world's finest Don Cherry impersonator, and Danny Z, a world-class mentalist. As you can see, the talent ranges from well-known and celebrated to the up-and-coming and soon-to-be-famous.

Since its inception, we have raised more than half a million dollars for the Calgary Veterans Food Bank. The format of the event—in common with most that I am actively involved with—has me paying all of the costs and soliciting charity cheques from attendees. One hundred percent of the funds raised go directly to the food bank. I feel very strongly about this cause because I don't believe our veterans get adequate recognition for the sacrifices they make in order that we can live in relative peace and comfort. Supporting our troops and veterans needs to be a year-round effort, not just something we do every November 11.

Here's what my friend George Bittman, who was chairman of Veterans' Food Bank before he passed away, said about the impact of our initiative:

> During the past number of Christmases, Brett Wilson brought world-class entertainment to Calgary for his benefit Christmas concert and generated more than $500,000 in donations for the Calgary Poppy Fund and Veterans Food Bank.
>
> These concerts were attended by a large number of veterans, many of whom were brought to tears by performances of the entertainers and the generosity of the audiences, who thanked them for their sacrifices while serving our country. In 2009, The Calgary Poppy Fund was one of the charities chosen to benefit from the FirstRowdy event—another firm and event that involved Brett. Once again the project was another extremely successful endeavour as the Poppy Fund received about $100,000.
>
> Due to the heightened awareness of the needs of our veterans, as they have been exposed by the efforts of Mr. Wilson and his programs, we believe our revenue has increased by approximately

$700,000 per year. The success of these two events has had a major impact on our organization due to the number of other groups and individuals who have selected the Calgary Poppy Fund as their charity of choice for annual fundraising events. Consequently we have been able to expand all aspects of our services to our clients, which is very important in the declining years of our veterans. In addition, we are now able to set aside funds for veterans' and seniors' housing, which we believe will become a major legacy to all Calgarians from our veterans. Thank you so very much, Brett.

The David Foster Gala

Early in 2007 I travelled to Phoenix to meet the celebrated Canadian musician, record producer, composer, singer, songwriter and arranger extraordinaire, the legendary "Hit Man," David Foster. He was interested in bringing an event for his David Foster Foundation to Calgary and his people had asked if I would serve as co-chair for the event, along with well-regarded Calgary businessman and philanthropist Wayne Henuset. Given the scope and scale of the undertaking (nine hundred people, black tie and at $1,500 per person the highest ticket price ever attempted in Calgary) I had told the event planning team that I wanted to meet directly with David to make sure that we were aligned with regard to values and expectations. We caught up in his Phoenix hotel room. He came to the door wearing runners without laces, jeans with holes in them, an untucked, rumpled, blue-linen, collared shirt, and he hadn't shaved in a few days. I looked at him—and laughed: I was wearing runners without laces, jeans with holes in them, an untucked, rumpled, blue-linen, collared shirt, and I hadn't shaved in a few days. We met for less than an hour and came to an agreement. His passion for entertaining and his foundation (which supports the families of children across Canada who are enduring the long recovery period that follows organ-transplant operations), along with a desire to bring a world-class entertainment extravaganza to Calgary were the hooks that caught my attention.

The original game plan had been to build an organizing committee of twenty to thirty people, and lean on each of them to sell thirty to forty tickets at $1,500 each. I was to provide a firm number on how many tickets I could sell. My response was undoubtedly why I was asked to co-chair the event in the first place. I said I thought I could sell only a few dozen individual tickets *but*, if they let me organize the marketing effort, I could sell all ninety tables. My reply was met with stunned silence. I reiterated my offer, explaining that I was certain that very few people—even in my circle of charity-minded business folks—would pay $3,000 a couple to sit at a random table, possibly with strangers. On the other hand I was equally certain, given the cause and offer (i.e., David Foster–led entertainment), that with Wayne's network and mine, we could find ninety people willing to step up to buy tables at $15,000 each. This would give them control over a full ten seats, and the associated opportunity for business development or goodwill that owning a table at a sold-out world-class gala would entail.

"*But*—how could I sell ninety tables quickly?" was the question next posed. David had offered to come to Calgary to do a private event—a teaser—to help sell tickets. He promised to bring along an unnamed someone to perform with him, drawing from his incredible circle of entertainer friends. Okay: game on! We organized a relatively intimate affair in June, an outdoor event under a tent in my backyard. We set it up for David and company to entertain, and then built an invitation list consisting only of potential table-buyers. Going into the event we had early, relatively firm indications of interest in about twenty-five tables. Wayne and I invited another 120 couples to attend, knowing we only had some sixty-five tables available. The momentum created that night by David (who slipped into town with nothing less than Clay Aitken from "American Idol" in tow) allowed Wayne and I to become order takers, selling out the event over the next few days. In less than a week, going from almost zero to ninety in car-driving terms, the event was a go!

We held the mid-September gala in two venues: the Hyatt down-town and the Jack Singer Concert Hall. We held the dinner in a theatere-in-the-round layout to allow all tables to be great tables. (I really don't enjoy events where the folks at tables at the very back of the room, far away from the stage, feel as if they should have stayed home!) Dinner and speeches were followed by a one-block walk downtown, all on red carpet under continuous tenting in case of rain, over to the concert hall. The logistics of moving nine hundred people from dinner to concert hall in a timely manner were an adventure in themselves.

David is a master at engaging his network to support his cause. He brought classic entertainers Lionel Richie, Peter Cetera and com-edian Sinbad (David Adkins) to our Calgary gala. I added Beverley Mahood and Kalan Porter to the lineup. The evening also included celebrity auction items, such as lunch with Donald Trump and ten-nis lessons with Andre Agassi. We even auctioned off one of David Foster's grand pianos, which was signed by dozens of his outstand-ing musical colleagues. The event was a tremendous success, raising $3 million—a record at that time—all in one night, for The David Foster Foundation.

Operation Western Front

Early in 2011, my good friend Warren Spitz and I organized a cor-porate dinner to honour the selfless service of our Canadian troops and raise funds for causes that support our military families. While the cause was serious, we wanted to make the event itself entertain-ing. The Vancouver Convention Centre was converted into a forward operation base and our guests experienced a simulation of a night in Kandahar and a meal in a mess tent. A helicopter hovered outside the ballroom windows to let reception guests know when it was time to enter the mess and take their army-style dinner trays to the buffet. In addition to black-tie and cocktail dress, guests were invited to dress in the colours and style of the military, which included safari and camouflage gear. Described by one local paper as "one of the most spectacular gala evenings ever to hit Vancouver," the event included emotional tributes to the fallen in Afghanistan by a host of artists and entertainers, and a spirited auction featuring the prime minister's wife, Laureen Harper, actress Shannon Tweed and her KISS front man Gene Simmons. The evening raised almost $1.5 million for military families and veterans in need and, more importantly, changed perceptions for many about the relevance and importance of our military families.

This event has its own Facebook page. I encourage you to find it for the eight-minute video tribute to the evening, which, along with pictures, describes the creativity and power of that evening better than words ever will. I intend to repeat the event in Calgary in due course, knowing that the depth of support there for our military is equal to that of any region in Canada.

Youth with a Mission: Homes of Hope

One of my two charity mentors in life is Sean Lambert, tireless founder of the organization Youth with a Mission (YWAM) San Diego/Baja. Founded in 1991, the organization grew in response to the need for affordable housing and other social service projects in the Northern Baja region of Mexico. One of their best-known projects is Homes of Hope. The story of Sean and YWAM deserves a book in itself. Check their website, www.YwamSanDiegoBaja.com, in which they share their story of building more than three thousand homes since the organization's inception.

Because home ownership is often the best way to break the generational cycle of poverty, Sean and his colleagues designed a simple, inexpensive standardized house that can be built by volunteers over a two- or three-day period. Measuring 16 x 24 feet (roughly 5 x 7 metres), and built on a simple concrete foundation, these homes offer their new owners hope in terms of breaking out of the lowest levels of subsistence poverty. Recipient families, who have to supply their own land and participate in the building project, get health benefits due to improved living conditions, increased emotional, financial and social stability, and better educational opportunities, which lead to more productive lives and communities.

I've now made the trip to Mexico nine times in the past twelve years to participate in the Homes of Hope building project. The experience is life-changing and it's been a fundamental part of my children's personal development. Rather than giving my kids a car to mark high school graduation (which many of my peers have done), I have funded trips for each of them, along with a group of their friends and classmates, to participate in the Homes of Hope experience. It has taught them a great deal about their potential for making a difference, and for engaging others in their own peer groups to do the same.

On other occasions, I have arranged to take friends and business colleagues along, totalling some fifty to sixty or even more people per trip. Together, we can now build three homes over the course of a three-day weekend—including travel time! In addition to the impact we make to the Mexican families we support, it's a powerful group-bonding and personal-growth experience for everyone who volunteers.

> "My own kids know that the vast bulk of my wealth will go to charity. I won't leave them destitute, but I also won't burden them with unearned wealth."—WBW

One of my best friends, Daryl Rudichuk, brought his son, Andrew, on a build a few years back. This young man came from an affluent family and, like many Canadian kids, had never really experienced or witnessed Third World poverty first-hand. At the end of the weekend, we all gathered around the family whose house we had helped to build. We were celebrating by presenting them with the keys to their new home. During the presentation ceremony, one of the family's children ran over and hugged Andrew, who turned to the group and said, possibly with tears in his eyes, "I have been fortunate to have lived a very good life full of travel and adventure, but let me be clear: this has been the best week-end of my life." What a blessing for him to see his personal potential for doing good—for changing the world—at such a young age. His testimonial alone justified my efforts to put the trip together.

Another group I have taken several times to Mexico consisted of kids and their parents from the Alberta Adolescent Recovery Centre (AARC), an addiction treatment centre founded by my great friend from university days, and the second charity mentor in my life, Dean Vause. AARC offers long-term treatment (averaging about a year) based on the premise that addiction is a disease. The program is often the treatment of last resort for young people who have been in jail, in front of the courts, suicidal, violent, in psychiatric wards, living on the streets, in other treatment programs and/or removed from their homes. AARC blends dedication and compassion with no-nonsense, uncompromising, honest confrontation in which clients and parents are expected to give as much as they get. Success at AARC is a gradu-ate who is clean and sober, back in school or working and reunited with his or her family. During the build, I got a chance to see fam-ilies, previously torn apart and almost destroyed by addiction, hap-pily working together. A hauntingly powerful memory for me was watching a father and son from AARC working side by side to shingle a small roof. No one could tell that at the depths of his addiction only a few short years earlier, the son had violently attacked his parents, and the father had risked his own life to save his wife from his son at that time. The memory of watching that father and son grow closer through the building process still brings tears to my eyes. Many youths who struggle with addiction have lived self-centred lives. The Homes of Hope project gave them an opportunity to focus on giving to others, and it became an important part of their healing process that will extend to their own communities when they return home. I know we will be making that trip again … and again.

What pleases me most about the Homes of Hope experience is that, in addition to helping dozens of families, YWAM has inspired people of means to use their network of friends and colleagues to do the same. A well-known Calgary entrepreneur, Tony Dilawri now brings his staff members back regularly, as does the inimitable business and community leader Sam Kolias. As more people see how easy it is to make a big difference in the lives of others, they engage their friends in the experience, and the circle of influence continues to grow.

Making this journey each year has been an incredible gift in my life and in the lives of my friends, partners and children. I urge everyone to take the time to experience the impact of this sort of hands-on work. At some point in your life, get on a plane with a group of folks committed to making a difference, and go to some corner of the world that needs help. Build a home. Bring some supplies. Help dispense medicine or clothing. Do anything. You may not be able to help everyone, but know that often the smallest thing you can do will make a big difference in the life of someone— and that someone might be you.

> *"To be content with little is hard; to be content with much is impossible."*
> *—Marie von Ebner-Eschenbach*

Outward Bound

In the summer of 1977 I discovered Outward Bound, a life-changing experience for me that I can recommend—with passion—to any teenager, as a voyage of self-discovery and examination, and confirmation that one's individual limits, both mental and physical, are far greater than most of us would ever imagine without testing them.

My Outward Bound experience was incredible. It was a month of hiking, running, climbing, camping, kayaking, freezing and cooking in the usually temperate August climate near Keremeos, B.C. I found patience, tenacity and teamwork skills hiding inside me that might never have been released without an Outward Bound experience. We encountered a freak August snowstorm, launched an extended search for a missing team member (who suffered hypothermia during the last night of the three-day solo excursion and wandered off before the morning check-in with our leader) and ran rapids upside down and backwards (oops!)—with my helmet scraping off rocks on the river bottom—until I could escape from my kayak, along with other team-building experiences I could have never imagined or experienced without Outward Bound.

I have been doing awareness raising and fundraising for Outward Bound for the last two decades. I have been sponsoring scholarships for students from my hometown in Saskatchewan and in the town of Strathmore, Alberta (where I have purchased a significant portfolio of real-estate development assets), to attend Outward Bound summer courses for the last few years. The thank-you letters tell me that my views on the value of Outward Bound experiences are shared by these students as well.

Wilson Centre for Domestic Abuse Studies

As a social worker, my mother, Doreen, was exposed to some horrific domestic situations. Our family often welcomed foster kids from challenging circumstances. These early experiences left a lifelong impression on me.

During the early days of FirstEnergy, we were often asked to support shelters for abused women and children. But I questioned how funding shelters really solved the underlying problems related to domestic abuse. Sheltering people from abusive situations is good, but I was more interested in stopping the abuse at its source, in finding ways to break the cycle of abuse.

To that end, I created and funded the Wilson Centre for Domestic Abuse Studies at the Calgary Counselling Centre. The Wilson Centre is now one of the leading research and treatment centres in North America for those affected by abuse. Their innovative programs provide the highest level of treatment to men, women and children who abuse or have been abused.

What sets the Wilson Centre apart is a proactive approach, with a focus on individualized treatment. Researchers at the centre seek the root causes of domestic abuse to help stop the cycle before it begins. People who go through the programs have among the lowest repeat-offence rate in North America. In the last six years, the centre has responded to approximately 7,700 requests for service, including counselling for men and women in domestic-abuse treatment, and treatment for abusive or aggressive children and youth. More than fifteen studies conducted by the centre have led to more than fifty invitations to make presentations at international conferences. In Calgary, the centre has trained hundreds of practitioners to recognize abusers and provide innovative and effective domestic abuse treatment.

In the future, the centre will continue to work to end abuse, with continued research on the relationship between addictions and abuse, decreasing the stigma of seeking help and accessing services early, whole-family healing and proactive work with men, women and youth to change behaviours before domestic abuse escalates.

According to Robbie Babins-Wagner, the CEO of the Calgary Counselling Centre:

> Brett's unwavering support for our work, including his financial and moral support, coupled with his understanding of the issue, have pushed us to think of domestic abuse in a broader way and have helped us to expand our focus to help men and women, youth and families, abusers and victims. Our role in ending domestic abuse, with Brett's inspiration, is a relentless push to find solutions to fuel lasting change for our clients.

The Seaman/Wilson Urology Centre Initiative

I first met Doc Seaman when I was working at McLeod Young Weir back in the late 1980s. I was invited to sit in on a meeting with Doc, but only after being warned by my then boss to "keep my mouth shut and listen." Even though he was a humble and unassuming man, he had a shock-and-awe reputation that commanded respect. He was also famous for his wince-inducing handshake. A fellow immigrant from small-town Saskatchewan, a fellow University of Saskatchewan engineer, a co-owner of the Calgary Flames and a leading player in the oil patch, Doc was an icon in the community and I deeply admired him.

In the fall of 2007, after the success of the birthday bash, I was delighted to be contacted by Doc regarding a major prostate cancer initiative. Even though we were thirty years apart in age, we were both prostate cancer survivors (or "graduates" as I prefer to say) and cared deeply about moving this cause up on the radar of donors.

Doc had been working for several years with the Calgary Health Trust to fund a new project, a state-of-the-art urology centre that would offer patients a one-stop shop for diagnosis, treatment and rehabilitation for a wide range of issues, including prostate health, kidney and bladder cancers, and incontinence. Every year, more than 2,400 men in Alberta alone were diagnosed with prostate cancer. The centre was beyond necessary. Doc had already indicated his early interest in donating upwards of $7.5 million of the $15 million that was thought to be needed to get the centre off the ground.

As we drove together to a meeting with senior people at the Calgary Health Region to discuss the new facility, I asked Doc if he would be willing to have my name stand beside his on this project. My suggestion was this: we could both provide $5 million for a joint donation of $10 million and use our individual networks to gain more profile and support for the initiative. For the promoters of the project, it was a step up from the $7.5 million and brought more than just cash to the table. "That works for me," Doc said quickly and quietly, and we shook hands. We knew that there was power in having one of the "old guard" join one of the "young bucks," and that together we would get the attention of the community and underline the importance of the project.

We launched the campaign with a high-profile public event featuring as our keynote speaker the inimitable American physician and social activist Patch Adams. His address, given in clown garb, helped to attract members of the Calgary philanthropic and health-care community, and significant media attention. Patch met with Doc and me in private to get a bit of background on our efforts. After shaking hands with both of us, Patch referred to Doc Seaman as "my fellow Doc" and, turning to me, smiled and called me "Doc Light." That worked for me, giving the stature of the men I was walking beside and behind. I'm proud to say that after announcing our lead gifts of $5 million each, many more individuals and groups stepped up, allowing the institute's $25-million price tag to be covered entirely by philanthropic dollars.

According to Bill Brooks, who at the time was director of fund-raising for the Calgary Health Trust:

> In any fundraising initiative, it's always hardest to raise your first and last dollar. Doc and Brett's major contributions paved the way for other like-minded philanthropists to follow their lead, and it helped us turn a fantastic idea into a reality.

Today the Southern Alberta Institute for Urology is a world-class resource for patients seeking a single-stop for diagnosis, treatment and rehabilitation for a wide range of serious urological issues.

Sadly, Doc passed away in January 2009. During his lifetime, he received wide and well-deserved recognition for leadership in business and for his outstanding charitable work. His legacy will live on through the many people he influenced, not least of which is another generation of philanthropists—including me.

The man in the portrait looks more puzzled than proud, secretly worried, as if circling a gnawing question that eludes its own answer.

It's there in the stitches of his sweater, the perfectly worn jeans, the attachment to flight, the willingness to prowl odd corners and make friends with dumpsters, the yen for discovery.

Explorer, engineer, originator. The choreograph of imagination, quizzical appraisal, responsive and perceptive. Clothes do not make the man but wait to gain life from their connection to the body that carries them.

The secret is that crease between the brows, watchful, evaluative. The stare, compelling, one that will not avert or walk away.

And who in the hell is peering over his shoulder? Wellington, or his arch-enemy Napoleon? No—some other uniform encrusted with braid, some pale campaigner longing to relax but trapped in the nineteenth century. Contrast, the portrait against the portrait, the un-portrait with its taste of character, its tantalizing kiss, its intense gaze fixed on the future more than the camera. A smiling enigma.

Airplanes or kites promise lift, the updraft that connects human to air, an ascent, a dream, goal, aspiration, and yearning.

There's the tenderness, plain as day, yearning and its tentative thread, following the kite string to mount a ladder of light, to discover a route hitherto untrodden, to capture the sun.

The man mans the portrait. He works his likeness.

—Aritha van Herk

Ten

Still Making Mistakes

Sharing one's life journey can be as exhausting as the journey itself. I appreciate anyone who has made it this far in my book. The goal of sharing my experiences has been to reveal the challenges I have faced and choices I have made along the way—and to inspire others to consider their priorities and choices. There is no doubt that the mistakes I have made along the way have influenced outcomes as much as my apparently wise choices. My investments, my choice of partners, even the arguments—some won, some lost—that I have engaged in, all have helped pave my path.

As I draw this book to a close, I want to share a number of what I call "Five Lists": lists of five items (or so) that are uniquely mine, reflect on where I have been, where I am now, and where I think I am headed. They show what inspires and excites me each day.

Five Favourite Investments

1. FirstEnergy Capital Corp. Building on the success of Wilson Mackie & Company, Inc. (my first business), I was one of four co-founders of FirstEnergy back in 1993. We started with just $2 million of equity capital. The business generated significant cash flow and enormous deal flow for reinvestment over the next

fifteen years, which formed the basis of other financial wealth I came to enjoy.

2. Penn West Petroleum Ltd. I was at the table when PennWest was reorganized in 1994: my original cost base was less than 20 cents per share; the stock has since traded in the mid-$20s, and now cash-flows more than $1 a share each year—an incredible long-term hold.

3. Meota Resources Corp. (a.k.a. Cheni Gold Mines Inc.). A partner and I took control of this entity when it was worth less than $1 million. Less than a decade later, we sold the company for more than $300 million (but not before attracting a top-notch management team, growing the asset base and issuing equity to the market along the way).

4. Pacalta Resources Ltd. Once again, I was at the table when Pacalta was reorganized: my investment was at $1.25 a share. The company was sold in a spirited bidding war for $13.25 a share less than four years later—and the stock of the acquiring company making the acquisition more than tripled in the ensuing decade. I am glad I still hold much of my original investment.

5. Maxim Power Corp. After learning to trade electricity in the potentially lucrative Alberta power market, a partner and I stepped up and bought 75 percent of the H.R. Milner Generating Station, a coal-fired power plant located in Grand Cache, Alberta. A year later we rolled H.R. Milner into the publicly traded Maxim Power in exchange for shares of its equity. We subsequently discovered that the coal-mining assets on lands that came with the power plant—once fully developed—will be worth considerably more than the entire company as it stands today.

6. Western Real Estate. (Okay, this is number six—I can count!) I have made a significant—to me—investment in farmland in Saskatchewan as well as in both developed and undeveloped real-estate assets in Alberta and British Columbia. As these properties begin to bear fruit, they appear to be on track as very wise choices.

Five Worst Investments

1. My First House. We paid $99,500 for a small home in northeast Calgary in May 1981. After the much-maligned National Energy Program coming into effect a year later, and in spite of investing untold hours and $20,000 in renovations, we eventually sold the upgraded home for just under $70,000 four years later. It was a great learning experience.

2. My First Restaurant. My partner and I invested almost $3 million getting the restaurant "perfect for downtown Calgary" off the ground. We were wrong—way wrong. There were innumerable challenges with menu and management, which meant missing budget continuously. We wound this entity up within five years, with value in the tax losses and little more. I have invested in the next restaurant to go into the same space, and that—knock on wood—appears to be the home-run investment.

3. Merit Energy Company. I was a co-founder at pennies per share. Rapid unfunded growth and management missteps took down this high-flying energy company, which once traded at $7 per share. Regrettably, Merit's final days were resolved via lawsuit and an out-of-court settlement. Oops.

Fortunately for me, nothing else in my experience comes close to the challenges of the investments listed above—so, yes, there are only three worst investments on my top five list (and hopefully it stays that way!). For sure there were lots of trading losses in the stock market, but these were more than offset by gains in other market cycles. Every loss resulted in lessons that proved invaluable in selecting or advancing other investments along the way.

Five People I Want to Dine with

1. Warren Buffett or Bill Gates. Frankly, I'd be happy to sit down with either one to review the thinking behind their ask to have billionaires commit to giving away 50 percent of their

      wealth—and discuss why I believe the ask is way less than it should have been.

2. Nelson Mandela. Simply to share the energy of the man who quietly tore up apartheid and began the process of healing a nation in a non-violent way, shaping the face of similar revolutions to come, would be a privilege.

3. Erwin McManus. This influential American pastor and lecturer has claimed that atheism is as relevant to spirituality as any religion. I would like to discuss this with him along with questions about God and the role of religion in our world. It will be a long dinner.

4. Elon Musk. I'd spend time with this inventor and entrepreneur in order to review and come to understand his simply brilliant decisions with respect both to business and philanthropy.

5. Winston Churchill. Okay, I realize this is a bit impractical, but I so admire his character and intellect, and the leadership he provided when the British Empire so needed comfort and courage. He closes my current dinner list.

Five Best Dragons' Den Deals

1. Hillberg & Berk Accessories Inc. This was my first deal in the Den—and one of the best. Rachel Mielke is focused, honest, creative and driven—a great partner—and the deal has generated healthy financial returns (as well as great jewellery for family and friends).

2. Frogbox Inc. One of the best pitches ever seen in the Den: Doug Burgoyne came to the studio wanting funds to expand his plastic-instead-of-cardboard moving-box company. He got the funds he needed and deserved. All is unfolding as it should, with more than twenty franchises in the system already.

3. 3twenty Solutions Inc. After telling Kevin O'Leary to "pound sand" in the Den, Bryan McCrea and partners convinced me that shipping containers could be readily—and profitably—repurposed

as remote housing camps. Sales are growing rapidly, markets are expanding and profits are coming.

4. The 7 Virtues. Barb came to the Den looking for capital and mentorship. She chose me as her sole Dragon partner after a few weeks of due diligence on the Dragons. The business—bringing essential oils for blending perfumes from war-torn regions of the world—is about empowering local suppliers to produce the oils (rather than contraband crops) needed for our unique "blended in Canada" perfumes. An exclusive distribution deal with The Bay was the launching platform.

5. Karoleena Inc. The Goodjohn brothers came to the studio looking for big bucks—but really needed mentorship and advice. In only a few short years we have restructured and refocused their business plan with a resulting order book approaching $20 million—a business worthy of nurturing as it might pay for all of my other Dragons' Den investments all by itself.

Five Regrets in Life

1. I regret not asking my grandparents (and others) for their stories—stories of their own grandparents and parents, and of the trials and tribulations of their life journeys. These stories now are forever lost.

2. I regret not taking the summer job supervising pipeline installation projects in Lebanon, which my engineering professor (and mentor extraordinaire) Dr. Karim Nasser offered me in mid-1976. I missed a great opportunity.

3. I regret not seeking common ground in my marriage sooner. By the time we started counselling, I don't think either of us was really committed to the process, which effectively doomed the outcome.

4. I regret not stepping into the Hoffman Process (an eight-day personal development program) when I first learned of it a year or more before attending. Maybe it wasn't the right time? For me the program was pivotal, enlightening and game-changing.

5. I regret not discovering and attending sooner The Meadows (or a similar program) to help me see clearly how out of sync my priorities were with my true values—the values of health, family and friends.

I voluntarily quit drinking alcohol the week I turned thirty. I chose to leave recreational drugs behind after high school. I have **never regretted** waking up after a night of being sober or straight. And I have never used drugs or alcohol as an excuse or reason for my actions. I hope each of you can always say the same after choosing to consume any combination of alcohol and drugs. There is no question that leaving alcohol and drugs out of my system had contributed greatly to my success—no matter how I define success.

Five Causes in My Future

1. Mental Illness. The wide-open field or world of mental illness is still the one we don't want to talk about. The cause needs spokespersons, people who will come out to share.
2. Eating Disorders. These constitute a group of causes that strike close to home for so many of us—including members of my extended family—and that desperately need funds and wider public support.
3. Aboriginal Entrepreneurship. I truly believe that exciting and encouraging the entrepreneur within each individual is key to establishing a sense of independence and self-worth for our First Nations peoples.
4. The Three Core Classes. I have shared my thoughts on the importance of teaching marketing, entrepreneurship and philanthropy beginning in elementary schools and continuing into all higher learning, either on the academic side or in the trades. Marketing is one's point of differentiation, while planting seeds of entrepreneurship and philanthropy will eventually change the world. Period.

5. The Serial Philanthropist. My final point here is that I will continue to seek out and support causes that are relevant to my family and me, causes which deserve awareness and funding, and that are often regarded as unmentionables or otherwise fly under the radar.

Five Great Life Moments

1. Kilimanjaro, Africa. I have climbed Kilimanjaro, Africa's tallest mountain at 5,895 metres, twice: once in 2001 for charity (and to celebrate the anniversary of the end of my primary cancer treatments a year earlier), and once with family in 2010. Both were incredible experiences. I will never forget calling my father each time by satellite phone from the top of that mountain.

2. Botswana, Africa. In the spring of 2007 I travelled for two weeks in Botswana with my daughters. We visited a number of exotic safari camps on a journey that culminated in an extended stay at Victoria Falls. We went river canoeing around hippos and my daughters went bungee jumping off of the 111-metre-high Victoria Falls border bridge. There were memorable experiences every day on this marvellous adventure.

3. Fiftieth Birthday Party. I have described in detail the events leading up to the 2007 Birthday Party that I put on jointly with twelve friends—all of us born in 1957—in support of prostate cancer. It was one of the finest events I have ever been involved with (but if you watch the video from Operation: Western Front, you will understand why I struggled with which of these events to choose).

4. Afghanistan. A highlight of my life was standing in a forward operating base near Kandahar, Afghanistan, serving Thanksgiving Day dinner to our troops in 2010. With the talented actor Paul Gross, the legendary hockey player Guy Lafleur, along with General Walter Natynczyk and Defence Minister Peter MacKay, I spent an emotion-packed five days in Kabul and Kandahar, creating memories that are often relived.

5.   South Africa. In the spring of 2012, I spent two weeks in South Africa. I saw everything from the Soweto and VryGrond townships to several game reserves on the west side of the renowned Kruger National Park, culminating with time in and around Capetown. The great white shark cage–diving experience may be my twenty-year-old son's and eighty-one-year-old father's most memorable moments.

6.   Galapagos and Bhutan. I have sailed the Galapagos Islands with my daughter and trekked in Bhutan with my son in the past couple of years. Both were quality-time experiences that I was fortunate to share with my children. (And, yes, that was *six* great life moments ... but wait! As the infomercial says, there's more! But I'll save those for another time.)

Five (New) Bucket List Experiences

1.   Storm Chasing. I would like to follow wild weather with a Canadian guide, somewhere in the tornado belt of central North America.

2.   Route 66. It would take only a couple of weeks start to finish, maybe in a '57 Ford Thunderbird—with a motorhome-based support team.

3.   Africa by Road. A tip-to-tip journey in about four months, starting in Cape Town, South Africa, and ending in Cairo, Egypt—or the other way around?—would be a magnificent adventure.

4.   Sailing Somewhere. I envision a voyage of three to four months— with decent internet coverage—maybe the Caribbean, maybe the South Pacific. Where can we still sail without the risk of encountering pirates?

5.   Around the World. But this is different: I want to touch, smell, feel, hear and maybe taste the ten largest slums of the great cities of the globe, from Africa to the Caribbean, the Far East to China and India. The population of slums is forecast to greatly exceed the non-slum-dwelling population of the world in the near future. Can I better help alleviate the suffering if I better understand what it's like?

Five Great Websites

1. www.TED.com. This is a collection of some of the finest inspirational and educational speeches in existence—each tightly timed to eighteen minutes—representing a cross-section of the globe's leading thinkers. I try to watch several talks every week.

2. www.BrainPickings.org. I use this website in the early morning to stimulate left- and right-brain thinking. I am fascinated by what I find: an hour here is far more rewarding than scanning news sites for often bad news and frankly irrelevant headlines.

3. www.PostSecret.com. I find this website captivating as a source of intriguing discourse under the guise of very public confidentiality. The combination of revealed secrets and incredible graphic design is cathartic at some level, and amusing and inspiring at another.

4. www.HowStuffWorks.com. For an engineer like myself, what's not to love about this website? This is where a family should spend time—instead of watching hokey reality television shows (other than uplifting business-related shows!). This is mind-expanding: take a look with family in mind.

5. www.WBrettWilson.ca. This is my website and so, of course, I am a bit biased. Take a look. You will find updates on the businesses and charities that occupy my life, as well as all sorts of connected press stories about my journey and people I have impacted.

Five Most Relevant Songs

1. "You've Got a Friend," James Taylor. This song was chosen by my family to play at my mother's funeral in 1987—her career as a social worker seemed to have been based on this song—because she was always available to be a friend for everyone in need.

2. "The Living Years," Mike & the Mechanics. This song is a poignant reminder of the relevance and importance of family. The significance of the lyrics became apparent to me during my participation in a program that is life-changing for many—especially me—the Hoffman Process.

3. "Highway of Heroes," The Trews. This song, which celebrates the respectful way that Canadians began to spontaneously honour those members of our military services who lost their lives in support of our freedom and country, strikes an emotional chord with me.

4. "Cat's in the Cradle," Harry Chapin. What parent would not be moved by the messaging embedded in this song? I would encourage everyone to read the lyrics every Monday morning as the workweek begins.

5. "Daddy Don't You Walk So Fast," Wayne Newton. A classic song sung by a great artist—its lyrics became relevant during the final years of my marriage. It hurt then—and still does—when I reflect on the impact of marital breakdown on the innocent victims—our children.

Five Key Bits of Business Advice

1. Three core life courses are key. Study marketing, entrepreneurship and philanthropy. I have emphasized it before—but the incredible relevance of these courses merits another mention. You cannot over-study these life courses.

2. Perfect-enough is key. Don't be limited by the wasteful and debilitating pursuit of perfection. That said, good-enough usually isn't good enough to win. The pursuit of perfect-enough will achieve acceptable success in almost every situation. Pursue a high standard.

3. Communication is key. I am not referring to social media. I am referring to internal team meetings, which must be held frequently and with an agenda—that agenda being everything relevant to your business. You need sharing and buy-in. Team meetings are critical.

4. Information is key. Never underestimate the relevance of paperwork. From business plans and financial statements to regulatory filings—you cannot steer your ship without the basic tools that information provides. Be organized—you can't plan the future without paying attention to detail.

5. Priorities are key. This book is predicated on this issue. Formulate your own definition of success and set your life priorities to achieve it. Priorities without passion are without purpose. Passion without priorities is wasted, or at best, misguided.

My list of Fives gives you a high-level summary of what is important in my journey, its past and present, and a glimpse of the future. The Fives idea came to me as part of the unique approach I took to my fifty-fifth birthday in the summer of 2012. I chose fifty-five key individuals from among my family, friends, staff and partners and gave each of them a cool, rugged high-end digital camera *and* asked each of them to direct $5,555.55 (of my money) to the Canadian charity of their choice. My way of celebrating a birthday, knowing there's nothing I need of material things, was to share what I have with my inner circle (and a few around the edges!)—impacting the lives of thousands more, we hope.

And From Here?

What is next? On the business and investment side, new opportunities continue to present themselves. Bruce Chernoff acquired the business of managing the largest closed-end mutual fund in Canada—EnerVest—midway through 2008. Shortly thereafter, given my recent retirement from active duty at FirstEnergy and our longstanding and very close friendship, he approached me to play a meaningful role in building on the significant cash flow that came from this management contract, with a view to building out a mutual fund company with national scope and scale. I respectfully declined—given that my plate was full—and that I had retired from FirstEnergy to focus on my own investments.

Bruce approached me again in the fall of 2010. He had attracted Nevin Markwart and Darcy Hulston to put a focus on growing the now newly named Canoe Financial LP into one of Canada's premier mutual fund companies, and had reached agreement with Bob Haber, a celebrated fund manager from Fidelity Investments, to manage the existing and new assets of Canoe Financial. This time the opportunity was compelling both from a financial and fun perspective. So I agreed to join as chairman of the firm, my involvement being to contribute significant capital to the balance sheet, and to devote time to developing and executing strategic plans for the company.

I am proud to say that since joining the reorganized firm in late 2010, Canoe has enjoyed the fastest growth rate of any mutual fund company in Canada. We are already in the top twenty asset management firms in Canada and expect to leapfrog over more than a few of our competitors in the next five years. We are already managing some $2 billion in assets and see that growing significantly over the next few years.

My time in television was a wonderful and almost vertical learning curve. In the fifty-five (coincidence?) episodes of Dragons' Den that I participated in for CBC TV, I am told that I managed to do more deals in studio than any other Dragon in the world. More importantly, as far as I can tell from publicly available information, I closed more deals than any Dragon in the world. In fact, I may have closed more deals than entire teams of Dragons in some countries. My approach was to take on a portfolio of deals—giving as many entrepreneurs a chance as possible—knowing many would stumble, but a few could and would thrive, and eventually pay for the entire portfolio. My handshake on the show was my commitment to find a way to do the deal in the real world, not just for TV. Would I do more television? I had a fun season with the Global/Slice television program *Risky Business* for sure, but the format needed more jeopardy and more time. However, shooting twenty episodes of one-hour programs was going to take almost two months of my life. Nope, I couldn't do it. I am watching for opportunities, ideally focused on mentoring or philanthropy. Many ideas have been proposed: at some point, something will stick, and I will happily return to the studio.

What else is next? My time spent speaking in public over the last three or four years has been fascinating. I have spoken on the same platform with folks such as Bill Clinton, Donald Trump and Martin Sheen. I have interviewed both former U.S. presidents George H. and George W. Bush, opened events for Ellen DeGeneres and Oprah, and shared my views on the importance of studying marketing, entrepreneurship and philanthropy with more than 100,000 teenagers via several of Free the Children's annual We Day events. I speak professionally to conferences and events about once a month, and will continue to do so with passion—especially when the audience involves our youth (or our troops).

> *"If you think you're going to do your children a favour by leaving them a big inheritance, think again. Inter-generational wealth transfer is one of the most serious issues of our time."—WBW*

Lastly, for me? My legacy will not be my journey on earth. It will be the three children I leave behind and the impact I have had on the lives I have touched, and intend to touch, over the many years to come. My dream is to continue to inspire others to be better, however that might be defined for them.

What is next for you? I would encourage you to reflect ever so briefly on my life experiences, knowing that I, too, put my socks on one at a time. I have been blessed with incredible highs and disappointing lows in my journey. I wouldn't trade them for anything. Then I suggest you take time, right now, to think about how you would define success: there can and should be many aspects or layers of meaning embedded in your definition. Then consider putting pen to paper to commit your definition of success to history, and follow with a list of your priorities, the things that are most important to meet your definition of success. Once you have shared your definition of success and your priorities with those you love, you are committed to a course of action that could change your life. It is all about choices now.

I love the quote "A successful man is one who has earned the respect and admiration of others." I would add, "especially that of his children."

Here is a man prepared to do battle with light.

Transportation, finality. Backstage of backstage, while the baton of the Calgary Tower pretends to flare and the street hums with oblivious action. Under the transept of the city, past horizons of skyline, the King Edward closed into its own acned brick mottled and shedding, graffiti-ready.

The blues echo quietly, blues in ballad and progression strumming a rhythm that speaks to the future. No one gets out alive but meanwhile, let's bend the notes to our purpose, play and play until we discover silence

And if there's a thread of melancholy, a fine back-vibration of regret, no attestation but in the quiet force of call and response, then listen carefully and play back to progression.

Here's a man on a corner, behind a derelict building but with a history shining with hope. A hotel for hope.

Here is how melody arrives: accidentals and frequency surprising discovery and its harmonics. Prompting melody and that impossible to isolate distillate that beams beauty.

Bent notes and grace notes, shuffles and walking bass, here is a man with a song all his own, attention turned to the finer points, those strings signs for performance, awareness, comprehension.

High-strung the sting and hustle of the city behind the wall. Pay attention, concentrate on that plucked string, that acoustic tone lamenting its echo. Scales and arpeggio in the life of a listener. Bridges enable vibration, and soundboard leads tone.

—Aritha van Herk

Afterword
by Keith Hanna

Inspiring People to Be Better

In the fall of 2009, I accompanied Brett on a series of speeches he was making in Ontario, the highlight of which was an event involving Donald Trump. This was not an unusual thing for me to do as his coach, since I am interested in how he performs in all aspects of life. Seeing him live in any situation is a great way to develop perspective, and there is nothing so revealing as a stage.

I had seen him speak for the first time in front of a large crowd in Calgary at a Power Within event. I had seen him onstage numerous times at smaller venues, but he had not really committed to being a professional speaker then. I had always known him as being funny and charming onstage, but he unleashed a new side of himself at the Power Within. He was so vulnerable, engaging and humble, rather than slick and polished; he had the people around me in tears as he told cautionary tales from his life in a fully transparent way that I wouldn't have normally expected to hear from such an accomplished person. I knew I was in for an interesting relationship with this man.

I didn't know who Brett was when I first met him. I don't get television where I live and I didn't travel in the oil and gas circles back then. He had developed a pretty serious following from appearances on Dragons' Den, and as a philanthropist and entrepreneur in Calgary, but I was fortunate to meet him, not as a celebrity, but just as a man—a man with all the normal aspirations and ambitions and ego and self-limiting habits that we all have.

At the start of his professional speaking career, Brett distinguished himself as an individual who would tell the unvarnished truth, about himself and about what he thought was going on in the world around him.

Just prior to his taking the stage in front of Trump in Ottawa, we were working on developing his influence. This might seem odd to some people who see him as the pinnacle of success in so any areas, but it's a testament to his authenticity that we were asking serious questions about it. He just knew he had more to give and he wanted to learn how to do just that.

We spent quite a bit of time developing a notion about what he considers his higher purpose and we arrived at the idea of inspiring people to be better. This idea is predicated upon the notion that people are more capable than they think they are. It's true of Brett as well.

What did being more influential really mean, and what would he do with it in Ottawa? What he decided in the end was that he would challenge the people in the audience to have a conversation that they were avoiding, whether it was with a friend, a family member or a business associate. It was a very simple challenge and people did follow through. He had at least three standing ovations during his talk and, in my opinion, which was shared by several members of the press, he stole the show from the headliner. I'm proud of him, of course, but what I like best is that he went and did what his higher purpose told him to do: he set out to inspire people to be better. And to do that, he had to become better himself.

A Work in Progress

In the classic movie *The Matrix*, Neo had his first meeting with the Oracle when he was trying to find himself. Above the door in her kitchen was the Latin phrase *temet nosce*, meaning "know thyself."

As a vocal proponent of coaching, Brett gave the keynote speech for the Calgary chapter of the International Coach Federation. A member of the press asked Brett why he thought he needed a coach, as successful as he is by almost any measure, and Brett simply said: "I don't know what I don't know." This insight has led him to several breakthrough personal-growth experiences, such as The Meadows and the Hoffman Process, and he is still an active member of the World Presidents' Organization, which is dedicated to enhancing personal leadership. He's come back transformed every time, with an enhanced commitment to further self-learning. He's done lots of work on his relationships with his parents and children, on his priorities and how he is learning to honour them, his mental health and his challenges with certain addictive tendencies. These investigations have all blossomed into a platform for doing good in the world.

Planting Seeds

I have had the pleasure and privilege of accompanying Mr. Wilson to dozens of charitable events across Canada. I realize that men of Brett's stature cannot create a positive impression on everyone they meet. Not everyone likes what he has to say and not everyone likes what he does. He provokes. He prods. He pushes. But I have always seen him to be a gracious and kind host, as he shares himself with so many fans and friends.

I was not particularly philanthropic when I first met Brett. I think this is true of many people when they first meet him. But over the years, I have learned the true value of making contributions to people less fortunate than myself. His invitations come with the request "Contribute something meaningful to you, and if you want to make it meaningful to me, double it." I have. He always says that giving is not an obligation but an opportunity. It's taken a long time, but I'm really starting to get it.

I believe accelerating giving while living is an important concept for people, for families and for the world. As we are facing the challenges of a growing population on this earth, I think entrepreneurs need to learn to see giving back not as a greenwash or publicity stunt, but as a true part of a sustainable business and sustainable communities. There are many challenges we face as a society, and, frankly, as a species; it really is up to entrepreneurs to answer the call—to get beyond the basic activity of making money and accumulating wealth and evolve into the more advanced business of making a difference.

I know Brett dislikes the idea of perpetual legacies. He often says that every legacy should have an expiration date and then that person's edifice ought to be cleared away for the next person and the next generation. I think his legacy is really about a very painful lesson he has learned about the pursuit of success at any cost. He's not the only one who had this same vision of material prosperity: the majority of people in the Western world have been pursuing a Gatsby-like vision of material success; the events since 2008 seem to be suggesting that the world is in the process of learning that lesson.

The Success and Happiness Paradox

It is of course potentially trite for someone who is quite wealthy and famous to criticize the pursuit of material success in favour of something more charitable. It would be trite if the lesson weren't so true.

What many successful people discover when they've achieved a degree of traditional material success is that it does not bring happiness with it. Brett learned the hard way that happiness in life and financial success in business are quite different concepts in reality.

Brett would say that his first phase in life was high on the happy scale but not particularly successful. Then something switched, and he entered his fame-and-fortune phase and became very successful but not nearly as happy. In the current phase of his life he is integrating happiness into a new definition of success.

Brett is the son of a salesman and a social worker. I think for him this integration was inevitable and, in the end, it led to a simple realization: happiness comes from giving and success from getting. It's really quite fine to have both, but neither lasts long without the other. Basic success is still material in nature: the achievement of meaningful business and professional goals, the pursuit of wealth to secure the well-being of the family and, of course, a few fun toys and adventures along the way. That is, at best, only one-half of the equation for a great life.

Happiness really rests in relationships with friends and family, taking care of one's health and spiritual needs, doing meaningful work and giving back to the community. These activities require neither fame nor fortune and truly recharge the processes of creating them. It only requires that people share the best parts of themselves with the people in their world. It's a very symbiotic process: giving and getting; loving and being loved; achieving and nurturing. For Brett, it's both a very big world out there and, sometimes, a very small one.

I spend quite a bit of time in Brett's beautiful office and with the team that takes care of his business pursuits. This is the coal face of the balancing act between the success and happiness processes. Pretty much everyone on the team has the word *fun* in his or her job title—there is even the manager of accounting and fun. This is cultural testament to the redefinition of success going on in his life.

The Challenge

The idea of redefining success rests on a central tenet: that success with happiness is the result of aligning daily actions and decisions with authentic personal priorities and principles. Brett, by his own admission, is far from perfect on this front. He still sometimes lets his ego make decisions on his behalf. He still says yes to things he ought to say no to, and is more overwhelmed with commitments than I would like. But I know he says no to a lot more things these days than he would have even a few years ago, and I see the results of his courage and leadership in his personal relationships and in the projects he undertakes. Many of these are hard decisions, including the ones relating to stepping back from television and, at times, his public career.

The theme of his growth at the moment is creating more order out of his personal chaos. This means designing systems and getting his team better organized to support the high-priority projects. This has required, among other things, that the ever-curious, highly detailed humanitarian and entrepreneur learn to see and take the simple path through the balance of his life.

So Brett does have a new definition of success. It's taken a few years to come to terms with it, but in the end, it's all very simple. Where he once defined success primarily in classic fame-and-fortune terms, he now defines success in terms of the most precious resource any of us has: time. Time to spend with bright and interesting people at the top of their game. Time to pursue entrepreneurial and philanthropic ventures he deeply cares about with people he deeply cares about. And free time for himself and his family and friends: the goal is to set aside three months of unburdened offline time per year, to be precise. (And feel free to remind him of that, if you ever see him.)

So I'll end with a question, because that's what Brett would do. We have taken an interesting journey in this book to arrive at a simple idea about how to live a great life on a foundation of personal priorities and principles that keep what is most important front and centre. So, what's something important to you, something that's not getting enough of your time? Maybe it's now time, to make some time, for that.

Keith Hanna is an executive coach with www.StepUp.net whose work is focused on Canada's leading innovators and entrepreneurs.

Royal Roads Commencement Address

Still Making Mistakes

This is the text of the Commencement Address given by W. Brett Wilson on October 26, 2010, to the graduands of Royal Roads University in appreciation of the bestowal on him of an honourary doctor of laws.

I am delighted beyond words to be here with you today. Partly because of logistics—I did leave Mumbai only yesterday, after one week in Afghanistan touring with our Canadian military and two weeks of trekking in India—but I am largely delighted to be here because of the incredible honour this recognition offers to me and my journey.

Now to formalities. Good afternoon, Mr. Chancellor, Mr. President, graduating students, ladies and gentlemen. And a special shout-out to a few folks from Saskatchewan who have joined me today, including my father, Bill Wilson, who was as surprised about this honour as I was, given that he is among the privileged few to know that in my fourth year of engineering studies, I failed Reinforced Concrete Part 2, not once, but twice!

I am very aware of Royal Roads' legacy as a great military school, and now as it moves forward with a close association with both the military and the community at large. I am especially appreciative and respectful of your school motto—"Living Our Learning"—and I promise to continue to live the personal oath I took when I finally graduated from engineering school, and that was, "I will never design a concrete structure larger than a bale of hay."

I have been asked to provide ten minutes, give or take, of "inspirational" conversation—which I am keen to do—once I answer the question that is burning deep within many of you: Is Kevin O'Leary really that nasty?

The answer: yes. And, no. To clarify: he is someone I really do enjoy working with—a great sense of humour and extremely bright—but not really someone whose chosen public persona or brand I want to align closely with. Poking fun at my social conscience, Kevin sometimes suggests that I add a teardrop to each dollar I invest. In retort, I have been known to suggest he is the moronic outlier of capitalism—truly one of a kind. We do really enjoy each other, both on and off the studio set. And I do appreciate that the combination of both nasty Kevin and friendly Brett apparently makes for good-to-great television. But, as you will understand if you have followed my way of working, thinking, giving, doing, there usually isn't room for both of us in a business deal!

Okay! Enough on the fantasy world of reality TV. Let's roam into the reality of the real world. You are graduating. You now know everything. Or almost everything. Or at least you know more than you did a few years ago. Okay, at least you know everything that you can remember!

In the time available, I want to share my perspective that choices and mistakes are the essence of life, that together choices and mistakes really do define your future.

Let me start with choices. I vividly recall watching a scene in a Harry Potter movie—*The Chamber of Secrets*—a number of years ago. I remember Harry and his sidekick, Ron, basically saving the world by breaking the rule about not going into the dungeon or cave below the girls' washroom and then slaying the vicious beast and the maniacal Voldemort. What was most memorable for me was the line used by the elderly headmaster, Dumbledore, when he was admonishing the boys in an almost admiring way. He chastised them for breaking the school's rules, but summarized with: "Men are not known by their abilities, but rather by their choices." This resonates for me when I reflect on the turning points in my life, and the fact that many could do anything I have done, but my life—my journey—is uniquely mine, because of the combination of choices I have made, both good and bad.

Now as to mistakes: I am working on a book currently entitled *Redefining Success in a Wealth-Obsessed World,* with the subtitle, which nearly caused my agent to have a heart attack, *Still Making Mistakes*. I am not ashamed of the reality that I am still making mistakes, hopefully fewer with time, hopefully not repeating many too often, and hopefully learning from them as I go. The key point I want to press here is that, for me, making mistakes is the precursor of success in every aspect of my life. In fact, not being afraid of making mistakes—the courage to face life as it comes—has been a choice I was able to make as I stumbled through adversity, from marital breakdown, to depression, to business and partnership failures, to cancer and addiction treatment … a ton of mistakes and a ton of learning.

I am fond of quoting, "the ability to make wise choices comes from experience, but experience comes from making mistakes." Now let me gather my thoughts in another way, by describing a few mistakes I encourage you to avoid, knowing they might be coming your way.

1. Please don't make the mistake of falling into the trap of defining success by material wealth, celebrity, accomplishment or power. I have been down each of those paths, and while fun for a while, they are superficial, lonely and not terribly rewarding. Success defined by the size of the car, the office or the wallet is fleeting. Success defined by the size of the smile—as a measure of happiness—can be the foundation or essence of a rewarding life.

2. Please don't make the mistake of running through life without stopping regularly to set—and even reset—priorities and action plans to align with those priorities. Just as a great lumberjack stops

to sharpen his saw, we need to stop to reload in life, for our sake and for the sake of those around us. Post my time in an addiction-treatment program in the spring of 1999, I took some time to look at my priorities. Post diagnosis with cancer a couple of years later, I then really took the time to establish clear priorities. My own very simple set of six life priorities is now as follows:

a. Health—all aspects of my health—emotional, spiritual, physical, intellectual—since without all of these on track life isn't going to be as much fun as it should be.

b. Family. I really encourage everyone to take the time to walk in the shoes of others in their family. You don't choose your family, but you do choose how you treat them, and how you respond to them. If things aren't quite what they could be in terms of family, try again. Try harder. But do draw a line at some point.

c. Friends. For me, friends are the essence of life. Friendships do vary with time and people—you already know that the more you give the more you get. You don't need a lot of friends, but you do need a few good friends. Remember that friendship is a two-way street.

d. Education. More on this later. I think education must be an integral aspect of your life journey for life to be meaningful and engaging.

e. Career. Whatever you choose to pay the mortgage, to make your mark outside the home, has to follow the other priorities I have just listed. And, yes, your career can consume a lot of time and energy, but don't let it consume you.

f. Community. Yes, this is last. I love what I do in terms of charity and community, but, yes, it has to rank last in a simple list of priorities for me, as the others need to be properly organized for me to be effective in each. These priorities get blended by demanding attention almost every waking hour of your life, but having a clearly defined set of priorities will help you allocate your time in a way that is best for you.

3. Please don't make the mistake of turning down or slowing down the learning curve, or of forgetting that you can influence the next generation and those around you with learning and teaching. My pet project: trying to convince schools, institutes and universities to include three courses, in an age-appropriate way, in the core curriculum of each educational program, to allow us to generate a new calibre of student. My list?

Marketing: I really believe you don't have a business of any kind without getting the order—closing the sale. Sure, you can *make* it, but if you can't *sell* it—so what? Understanding the value of brand, goodwill and the purchasing decision-making process is an invaluable competitive advantage over others, even when it comes to preparing your own resumé and business card.

Entrepreneurship: The great debate: are entrepreneurs born or are they made? I am here to share the answer—*yes!* There is no question some people or cultures are predisposed to seeking out entrepreneurial opportunities, but I fundamentally believe that entrepreneurs are not thrill-seeking risk-takers, but rather—by virtue of their experiences—they simply view risk differently. Studying examples and experiences of great Canadian entrepreneurs can plant seeds that will bear fruit decades later. Dragons' Den is planting the seeds that tell a generation of our youth that regardless of their vocation/education, they, too, could be in business someday for themselves. And,

Philanthropy: For me, this is a world of great opportunity, the world of charity/community/giving—whatever you call it. I take exception with the concept of corporate social responsibility, as I think that anything we do out of a sense of obligation or responsibility is done without the passion or enthusiasm that comes with seeing something as an opportunity. I do fundamentally believe that giving back is an opportunity, an opportunity to change the world you and your family live in, to improve the brand of your business, to invest in the future. Period. Should giving be altruistic? What act or action is truly altruistic? How do we foster and feed a social conscience? Why do we transfer any wealth? Why not distribute wealth while we are living? All questions without simple answers—and all worth discussing at every stage of life.

Okay, to conclude, you now know I have a book coming. You could Google me to find videos on my core life and business messages. But you can skip the book and Googling me if you were really listening today. In essence, my core messaging is very simple: remember, it's all about choices, and not being afraid of making mistakes. In fact, embrace mistakes as they accelerate your learning curve—and lead to better choices.

As you leave Royal Roads, I remind you of J.R.R. Tolkiens' quote that I encourage everyone to respect: "Not all those that wander are lost."

I encourage you to always seek to answer the question: What can I do with my knowledge, my network, my passion—basically my choices—to meet the world's greatest needs?

I promise you that no matter your skill set or abilities, it will be your willingness to believe in yourself, to bet on you, that will literally change your world and thus our world, one small but meaningful step at a time.

Thank you again for the wonderful honour of this recognition. I am proud to be associated with Royal Roads University, and in particular with the Graduating Class of Fall 2010.

Photographic Art and Words Explained

When you read the background information below and scan the pictures (actually art!) by Cynthia Robinson and the associated "word/poems" (or riffs as she also calls them) by Aritha van Herk at the beginning of every chapter you will understand and hopefully appreciate why I and the team behind this book felt compelled to include them.

CYNTHIA ROBINSON is a Canadian photographic artist from Goderich, Ontario, who now lives and works in Calgary, Alberta. Cynthia enjoys composing using many mediums, but perhaps above all she appreciates the complexity and rectitude of photography.

Why Brett?

I wanted to present Brett in a way that I had never seen him shown. A little darker. A little edgier. Brett is irrefutably positive so I was not at all certain how he would feel about my vision for this shoot. He told me, "Don't explain it. Just do what you do." And that is what I did. I could not be more pleased with Brett's versatility nor with the resulting photographs.

ARITHA VAN HERK is the author of fiction, non-fiction and public commentary, including hundreds of reviews, articles and historical narratives. She has written five novels, *Judith*, *The Tent Peg*, *No Fixed Address* (nominated for the Governor General's Award for Fiction), *Places Far From Ellesmere* (a geograficione) and *Restlessness*. Her irreverent Mavericks: An Incorrigible History of Alberta frames the permanent exhibition on Alberta history at the Glenbow Museum in Calgary. *In This Place* (with George Webber) develops the idea of geographical temperament as tonal accompaniment to Calgary; she augments Webber's haunting photographs as well in the collaboration *Prairie Gothic* (2012). She was artist-in-residence at the 2012 Calgary Stampede. She is a professor of English at the University of Calgary, Alberta, the recipient of many awards, a Member of the Alberta Order of Excellence and a Fellow of the Royal Society of Canada.

Why Brett?

Why do we read autobiographies? What do we imagine about public personages? What do we believe motivates those individuals, and how do we read them, from close up or from afar? In truth, we invent public figures, endow them with our own imaginings, sometimes enviously, sometimes erroneously, sometimes generously. We are, within the culture and framework of lives lived large, voyeurs and critics, gadflies and gawpers, fans and admirers.

I cannot claim to know W. Brett Wilson at all. I wrote the poetic riffs in response to the photographs for his autobiography from a position of intense and curious myopia, even blindness, knowing "about" his activities, but knowing in actuality not much about the facticities of his life. I knew his reputation as the generous Dragon on Dragons' Den. I know that he continues to practise an extreme philanthropy that dares every Calgarian and westerner to invest in community with the same passionate flair that he does. I know for certain he is a challenger, one who makes those who come into contact with him question their own energies and motivations. That makes W. Brett Wilson interesting to me—and to many others. He is a watchable man.

In my writing and in my life, I am persistently tempted by the tension between public and private. As a writer and cultural commentator, I am fascinated by the extent to which humans are subject to historical and geographical and economic forces. I consider it part of my artistic role to address those elements of torque, for they shape character. Finally, as someone intensely interested in performativity and influence, I consider myself to be a literate voyeur, participant as audience and collaborator, pundit and provocateuse. And of course, I work with words, my medium of choice. My daily joy is to put words to images, events and ideas, and in the process to make people appreciate and value language, that most taken for granted and yet indescribably complex tool. We connect with one another through language; we need language's clarity and complexity to understand one another.

When Brett Wilson asked me if I would be interested in providing some creative "commentary" for his images, I hesitated because I do not know him. But having seen his many countenances, their suggestive resonance, I could not resist. The gift of this project for me has been coming to understand that autobiography and picture and poetic riff are all part of a colloquy with time, with playful character, and with ideas, creative and invented and starkly real.

The riffs on these portrayals of the enigmatic and intriguing W. Brett Wilson then are a conversation, with him certainly, but also with those who might look at a photograph and imagine that what they see is simple. It never is, for every image contains elements that are mythological, allusive, elusive, gestural and deliciously duplicitous. Years ago, Rod Stewart reminded us that "every picture tells a story." In truth, every picture tells a multitude of stories.